"Our Toilets are Not for Customers!"

...by Floyd Coates

I hope you enjoy reading this book as much as I
  enjoyed writing it.

What Kind of book is it?

It is the story of my life.

It is a book to help you by my mistakes.

It is a book on how to treat the customer.

You may laugh, you may cry.

You may say this guy is nuts.

You may learn to understand and enjoy life in a
  different way.

PUBLISHED BY WING AND A PRAYER
Copyright © 2000 by Floyd E. Coates

ISBN 978-0-9678624-0-8

First printing	5,000	January 2000
Second printing	20,000	August 2000
Third printing	5,000	April 2001
Fourth printing	5,000	March 2002
Fifth printing	5,000	September 2003
Sixth printing	5,000	August 2005
Seventh printing	5,000	September 2006
Eighth printing	5,000	February 2008
Ninth printing	5,000	November 2008
Tenth printing	6,000	March 2010

Printed in the United States of America

Printed and bound by:
Old Paths Tract Society, Inc.
Shoals, IN USA

ATTENTION: SCHOOLS AND CORPORATIONS

Wing And A Prayer books are available at quantity
discounts with bulk purchase for educational, business, or
sales promotional use. For information, please write to:

Special Sales Department,
Wing And A Prayer, Inc.,
965 South Elm Street,
Scottsburg, IN 47170.

Please supply: title of book, ISBN,
quantity, how the book will be
used, and date needed.

Table of Contents

Introduction

There are two ways to study customer service. The first is with anecdotal evidence. The second is with theory, authority and principles behind good customer service. This book intends to do both.

What follows in the first part is a set of good and bad examples of customer service.

This book is dedicated to the essence of customer service. But, the question is, "Who is the customer?" What relationships fit the customer/supplier model? When you approach life with the view that every person is the customer, you begin to realize that you need to spend each moment of your day trying to satisfy his needs.

The relationship could be:

Customer	Supplier
Employer	Employee
Taxpayer	Government Worker
Parent	Child
Master	Servant

Student   College

Patient   Doctor

Others   Self

In our relationships with our customers and in all other aspects of life, if we concentrate on getting rather than giving, we will be sorely disappointed.

When you look at each transaction between people as a customer/supplier relationship, you can learn to grasp what is the right thing to do. Is the supplier really trying to serve? Is the customer being served? The book that follows is an attempt to illustrate some of those customer/supplier relationships.

I was taught early that we have a responsibility to love God and to love our fellow man. God's standard for customer service is quite clear: "Servants, obey in all things your masters according to the flesh; not with eyeservice, as menpleasers; but in singleness of heart, fearing God: And whatsoever ye do, do it heartily, as to the Lord, and not unto men; Knowing that of the Lord ye shall receive the reward of the inheritance: for ye serve the Lord Christ."

7 habits of...

I have been told:

There are 7 habits of joy.

There are 7 habits of success.

There are 7 habits of a happy marriage.

There are 7 habits of everything.

Because I wanted to be successful, happy, handsome, smart, rich, I determined to list my habits. I had only five.

1. Sleep late every morning.

2. Always drink cold Pepsi with pizza.

3. Pray daily.

4. Speak to my wife first each day because if I do not, I will never get in a word edgewise.

5. Run for Congress every 2 years.

2 laws of Life

I then realized that my habits were really driven by the 2 laws of life. What are these **2 laws**? They are not new with me. They were written 6,000 years ago by Jesus Christ.

I. Love God.

II. Love others.

If I love God I will certainly love His creation and the beautiful stuff that is in it. If I love God I will love life; I will be a participant not an observer. If I love life I will not see hardships, just hurdles. There will not be mistakes but lessons. There will not be bad people but just folks who do bad stuff because they have not found God yet.

If I love others, I will be constantly thinking how I can make the lives of others better, make them stronger, more comfortable, and more free.

So the remainder of this book will be used to measure my life against the **2 Laws of Life**.

Some people wait around for others to write their life's story. What if a man lived all his life and nobody bothered to tell the rest of the world what he had learned? That option is risky. Should what I learned only be revealed fifty years from now, after I am no longer on earth? I have chosen to write mine now. That way, I can say what I want and leave out the details that are not so flattering. With that as the basic premise, here is my account of my venture into the world of life.

Living life on the edge has become one of the greatest teachers of my life. It is not the wind that blows but the set of the sail and the till of the rudder that determine our destiny. When I was nine years old, I did not know what God had in store for me. I did not plot out my life on a grand scale. I did not draw a chart to hang on a wall to plot out my progress.

Somehow in my immaturity I found the wisdom to realize that, while standing in "valleys of decision," I should always make the choice which is morally and civilly right. As you will, so it shall be. Here follows my story:

1

The Writing of an Epitaph

Of course, I did not waste money as a kid. There was no money. At least I did not get any until I was ten. My father believed in discretionary spending for children and gave me twenty-five cents per month. When cash did finally appear in my life, I hung onto it tenaciously; I saved cash and preserved resources as if there would never be any more.

Age 10

I learned early to save as much money as possible. I constantly thought this question, "Do I really want this thing more than I want the option of maybe purchasing something better later?" I learned to say "no" to myself.

By age ten, the principle of helping other people with no expectation of reward was well established.

> **I learned to say "no" to myself.**

Age 13...first business

By age thirteen, I had developed some knowledge and experience with electricity. I had developed the skill of being able to install new electric cords on appliances such as toasters, irons, and lamps.

At age 13, one afternoon I was lying in my bed and the following thought occurred to me:

I am poor, ignorant, ugly, and I have no friends.

The epitaph on my tombstone would read, "He lived, he died, he did not make any difference."

I thought about that and wondered, could I change those things. If so, how?

I noticed a characteristic of rich people; they had money. I also noticed that poor people did not have money. I noticed something else, both rich and poor handled money, but the poor people seemed to spend one hundred percent of that which they received. Rich people however, had the characteristic of spending less than what they earned. As a result, I developed the principle of saving twenty percent of what I earned. The savings resulted in postponed purchasing power. I continued the habit of saving twenty percent of my income from age thirteen.

I was also ignorant, but I decided I could fix that. I started reading the encyclopedia from cover to cover, because I thought they had all knowledge in them. I started to read from the letter "A" through about four and a half volumes of the encyclopedia to "electricity." I then went to the local library, checked out more books on the subject of electricity, and read them. I was now on the way from ignorant to learning.

Age 16

Three years later, at age sixteen, I became a Christian. The pastor, Bob Wiggs, explained to me that ten percent of my income should go to God and His work. I reasoned if ten percent is good, twenty percent must be better, so I started contributing twenty percent of what I earned to God and His work.

God can do quite well and survive quite well without my cash contributions; however, through the giving of twenty percent of my income to the work of God, I develop the characteristics of self-control and generosity.

As a teenager, I remember my mother daily giving me thirty cents for lunch at school. I remember purchasing four bottles of milk and eight peanut butter sandwiches each day. Those only cost me eigh-

> **That left me twelve cents per day for savings.**

teen cents per day. That left me twelve cents per day for savings.

For the successful capitalist, self-control is an essential major characteristic. At this time, God was getting twenty percent of my income, savings was getting twenty percent of my income, government was getting thirty percent of my income through taxation, and I lived on the rest of the money. At first, this was not a very high quality existence, but after a period of several years, I was able to become comfortable with the habit of living on less than I earned.

When I was fifteen other boys my age were going to the local swimming pool and splashing around in the hot afternoons. My father, a believer in slavery, suggested that I work in his newly started business of molding plas-

> # For the successful capitalist, self-control is an essential major characteristic.

tic. As a youth, I learned to follow my father's suggestions. He was short of cash and paid me ten per cent of the minimum wage. His factory, however, provided me the opportunity to learn how to sweep floors, clean toilets, wash windows, and do all sorts of menial tasks. After a few months, I was permitted to learn how to mix plastic raw material and clean the machinery, and later to operate production equipment. Even though my wage level was now one-fifth the wage level of adults working in the factory, I gained the unique skills necessary to operate the machinery.

Two years later I began to receive the rate of pay equal to the adults working in that plastic injection molding plant. Even though my wage level was low, I continued the habits of saving twenty percent for myself and contributing twenty percent to the church.

By age sixteen, I purchased my own car, insurance, and tools to fix it whenever it broke down. Lying underneath the car beside the road was not an uncommon occurrence. In those days, it took a mechanic to drive a used car, and I became one.

Virginia Military Institute

I attended Virginia Military Institute for one year. Then I worked full time for one year and bought a new car. The next school year I continued at Hanover College. It was that year, 1964, that I loaned my father $2,800 to help him start another plastic molding company. (I married Sandy in 1965; she died of cancer in 1994.)

I continued to work part-time on evenings and Saturdays doing cost estimating. I continued to earn money while going through school.

My father insisted that any future leader of his company would be a college graduate. However, even after I became a college graduate, he wanted to continue to pay that graduate minimum wage. As a result, I went looking for a job elsewhere. By the time I had graduated with a Bachelor's Degree in Physics, I had accumulated an equivalent of three or four years of experience in plastics and ended up receiving the second-highest dollar amount job offer of any student graduating from that college that year.

Dad then realized that his best employee would no longer be around to do most of the work, so he gave me a raise to slightly higher than what the DuPont Company had offered. Two years later, Dad decided to sell the company.

Age 27 Fired

Two years after the sale the new owner decided to terminate my employment. At that point, I had a problem.

Having been fired from a steady secure job, I needed to either find another job somewhere or start my own business. I figured that starting my own business would actually be easier than facing the psychological defeat of looking around for a job paying what I thought I was worth and not being able to find one.

I had $3,000.00 cash saved up by this time, which was the equivalent of approximately three month's wages. I located a telephone company that needed electrical connection terminal blocks molded out of polystyrene. The manager told me that if I could mold them, he would give me the order.

I took the $3,000.00 that I had saved, and made an agreement with the owner of a plastic molding machine to rent to me his machine for $150.00 per month. By the use of his machine, I was able to manufacture plastic parts, which I then sold to the telephone company.

They were so happy with what I produced that they gave me orders to produce additional products. Within months, I became so busy molding parts that I needed to operate my plant twenty-four hours per day and hire other people to help.

Our company's sales continued to grow so much that we purchased ten acres and built a building which has since been expanded several times. Now it covers over 100,000 square feet.

We now employ approximately 130 people with sales of approximately twelve million dollars to over two hundred customers. American Plastic is no longer always the lower bidder but rather a quality and service leader in the industry.

2

Louisville Disappears from Earth

This story begins in about 1969 when I started to fly. My instructor, Frank Robinson, told me several things, some of which included: never stall an airplane below 1000 feet; never fly when you can't see. He also told me that there are old pilots; there are bold pilots; but there are no old, bold pilots.

In July of 1971, I was fired from a steady job. Being unemployed, I decided I had better resume providing for my wife, daughter and mother-in-law.

It was time to quickly launch into my own injection molding of plastic business.

I decided it was about time to start making some practical use of the fun airplane which I owned, a 1949 Stinson Voyager, November 8181 Kilo. I set out on a sales trip to visit people whom I thought I could serve by providing them with injection molded plastic parts.

After calling on a prospective customer in Dayton, Ohio, I came back to the airport, preflighted the airplane, and then took off. Part of the preflight procedure, of course, for early that morning had included draining the water out of the fuel tanks—water that sometimes condenses in a partially filled gas tank. Because I had done that in the morning, I did not repeat that part of the checklist in the afternoon.

Engine sputters...

After having the gas tanks filled, I took off from the South Dayton airport. As I climbed out, about one-quarter of a mile from the end of the runway, the engine started spitting and lost power. Because of the plane's velocity, the propeller continued to windmill, but there was no power. I said to myself, "Ah, this is an excellent time to make a sharp U-turn and put this thing back down on the runway!" Following emergency procedures, I switched gas tanks suddenly from the right tank to the left tank; the engine coughed, took life, and began to run again. I realized instantly that probably there was a fuel problem, likely a plugged up fuel line in the recently filled right tank.

Just after I decided to circle the field and land, the engine sputtered again. I said to myself, "Self, there's Interstate 71 on the south side of Dayton. You'd better land on it." At this time of day, the traffic was bumper to bumper and it looked like an un-fun experience to land between the cars. I decided to try to sneak back to the airport. Sure enough, I had enough height and speed to safely land the airplane, coast it to a stop and check out the problem.

Water in gas tanks...

I got out my drinking glass and drained some liquid out of my fuel tank. I found about a half glass of water in my tank. Apparently in the airport's fuel tanks, water condensed, and I happened to be the lucky customer who, while having gasoline pumped into my tanks, got just enough water to cause the engine to quit. Well, I took my approximately half a glass of water in a glass with gasoline on the top of it back to the guy that sold me the gasoline. I told him I'd appreciate it if he wouldn't sell me as much water the next time. He didn't seem to be too sympathetic about my problem. I drained the rest of the water out of the tanks and took off. Thankful for having this sort of experience close to an airport, I figured the rest of my trip would be uneventful.

Engine power drops...

It was, that is, until I got near Beckley, West Virginia. Suddenly engine speed dropped from 2300 rpm to 1900 rpm. I began to descend. I said to myself, "Self, this is a bad situation, because in addition to putting water in my fuel, this person probably put trash in my fuel. Now there is something plugging up the fuel filter or the carburetor. Any second now, it will be completely plugged up, and I will be needing to find some place to land among these trees and hills." I was just barely able to maintain the altitude I was flying. I got on the radio and called for help.

I said, "Help, folks, I have engine problems. This is 8181 Kilo and I want to land on the closest runway."

I was able to hang the airplane to the sky until I had the airport in sight. You cannot imagine the quantity of relief I had when I flew the plane over the runway. Getting ready to land, the man called me on the radio and said, "8181 Kilo, we appreciate your emergency situation but we think you're a little bit high."

I replied, "I know; I like it that way."

He called back and said, "The last guy that came into this airport as high as you are ended up overflying the entire airport, running over the end of the runway and falling off the edge of the mountain." In my super concern for staying as high as I could for safety's sake, I had failed to lower myself down to the appropriate approach altitude. I realized I had better lose some altitude quickly. I decided to do steep spirals over the end of the runway, and was able to grease it down onto the runway. I stopped close to the end of the runway where a previous pilot went over the edge. I donned my mechanic's uniform and soon found the culprit: fouled spark plugs.

Two emergency landings in one day is all this kid could stand. I said to myself, "Hey, it's already six o'clock in the evening; let's bed down for the night. Let's let tomorrow handle some of tomorrow's problems; don't solve any more today."

Fog in the mountains...

The next morning, knowing I was well behind schedule, I got up at four o'clock and went over to the airport well before sunrise. I looked at the weather and said, "Hmm, fog. Fog. This is dumb." Nevertheless, being a bold, young pilot, I decided to take off through the fog. After all, my thought was, the engine probably won't quit. I decided I would run the risk of taking off through the fog. The problem, taking off through fog, is if your engine quits, you can't see to find a good place to land. But being long on faith and short on judgment, I took off. By the way, did you

> **Did you know that good judgment comes from experience and that experience comes from bad judgment?**

know that good judgment comes from experience and that experience comes from bad judgment?

I took off, got on top of the fog and everything was fine except now I couldn't figure out where I was because I couldn't see anything under me except whiteness. I headed in the proper direction, climbed up and got over the mountains. By the time I got to Ranson, West Virginia, the clouds had cleared and everything was fine. I visited with the prospect there, flew on down to Raleigh-Durham, North Carolina, visited with a customer there and took off for home.

That was a wonderful afternoon, problem-free. I had been flying a lot that day and enjoying the wonderful sunshine and absolutely clear sky, no bad weather for a million miles around. Nobody was on the radio because there was nothing to talk about as far as weather was concerned. In my boredom about every fifteen minutes I'd call up flight service; I'd ask them what the weather was like. Their response, "Clear, no problem, and nothing reported, no weather, fine clear, clear, clear, clear." This went on for hours it seemed.

The storm...

I was within about ten miles of home, I thought, when I saw one little old cloud pop up ahead. What do you do when you have just one little old isolated cloud? Either you fly around it or you fly through it. Since I had never flown through a cloud before, I thought I would try it. Straight in I went. Suddenly, total whiteness surrounded me. I mean there was white up, white left, white right, and white down. I was looking around shaking my head from one side to the other and craning my neck to try to see something besides whiteness. I forgot which way was up and which way was down. I began to experience vertigo. I asked myself, "Just which way is up? Is it that way,

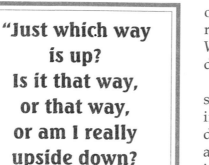

"Just which way is up? Is it that way, or that way, or am I really upside down? Where am I? What am I doing?"

or that way, or am I really upside down? Where am I? What am I doing?"

Uncertain, not having spent much time on instruments before, I didn't really trust them, and even though the instruments were pointing "this way" for up I really knew up was that way, and I would begin to turn. "But why is the compass turning the other way? Why is the magnetic compass turning this way and the gyro compass turning the other? And I really feel... which... What am I doing?" My thoughts tumbled over themselves.

Then the words of my instructor came back when he said, "Whenever you get into a situation like this, make this needle on the turn bank indicator point to this position right here and hold that position for one minute. After one minute you shall be going the way from which you came."

That's exactly what I want to do, because I want to get out of there. 'Cause this idea of flying when I can't see just was not quite as appealing to me as I first thought it would be. I made the turn and then leveled out. I realized, "Yes, I do have a compass heading of approximately 180 degrees from what I had when I entered this turn." After another minute or two, I was out of the cloud.

I was scared to death, nervous, sweating, tired, and worried when I realized I had less than fifteen minutes of daylight left. I thought, "I'd better fly to an airport and land. Forget about going home. Don't get killed by what's called get-home-itis (the uncontrollable urge to just get home just because it's safe there). It's not safe there. It's not the place to go."

There is another rule: Always have options, and exercise those options while you have them.

Exercise options while you have them...

I asked myself, "Where can I go?" Well, the last airport that I remembered seeing was too far away, and I'd get there way after dark. I did not have enough fuel to get there, and there were no other airports close. "I think I had better exercise my options while I have them, and I had better do it quickly." I selected a cornfield.

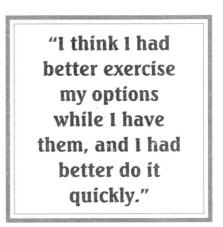

"I think I had better exercise my options while I have them, and I had better do it quickly."

Cornfields are great for landing airplanes. They do something for you. With August's eight-foot-high cornstalks, you slow down very, very quickly. You generally do not slow catastrophically, and you do not kill yourself but you sure do tear up an airplane. Since this was the only airplane I had, I really did not want to do that.

"Which is better, to die and ruin your airplane, too, or just ruin your airplane and walk away from it? Surprise. Right next to the cornfield is a soybean field. Yes, soybeans are much more fun to land in." I was about ready to lay it down on this bean field when an interstate highway popped up. I thought it was Interstate 71 between Cincinnati, Ohio, and Louisville, Kentucky.

That was great. I said, "That is a far superior landing runway than I could ever ask for; why don't I just land on it? But wait, but wait, it goes straight to Louisville. Ah yes, yes, there is Louisville." Well by now, of course, it was dark. Now I could see the lights of Louisville, thousands, millions, trillions of them — almost as many lights as there are dollars in the government's debt. I decided, "Yes, I'll just follow this on in to Louisville."

I decided to contact the flight service station and tell them about my dilemma. I called up Louisville flight service, "This is Stinson 8181 Kilo and I'm basically lost. I am low on fuel, over the mountains of Kentucky at night, and I do not do much night flying. I am tired, and I was wondering if you could tell me exactly where I am. I'm over an interstate highway that has a railroad just to the north of it and I think it is Interstate 71." He tried for ten or fifteen minutes to find me on radar and could not. Turns out I was just above Interstate 64 between Lexington, Kentucky, and Louisville, instead of Interstate 71 between Cincinnati and Louisville. We had several exchanges of conversation until he finally decided where I was.

Detecting nervousness in my voice, he asked, "How are you doing?"

I told him, "Kinda fine." But I wasn't liking what all was going on.

Louisville disappears...

Terror struck.

This is when I thought Christ's Second Coming had occurred because Louisville disappeared. I thought I had missed the rapture of the saints. Louisville appeared to fall off the face of the earth. I went into panic at this point.

I could see the remnants of little lights in the country, all the way under me, behind, everywhere, but Louisville just disappeared. I said to myself, "God must have put His judgment on this city. I am tired; I am low on fuel; I am hungry; I am confused; I am somewhere where I should not be; and the city has just disappeared. I have problems. Do something. Land this thing while I still have options."

I called the man on the flight service and said, "8181 Kilo, I'm thinking that I'd better get this thing on the ground because I don't like what I'm seeing because Louisville just disappeared."

The man from flight service called back and said, "8181 Kilo are you IFR?" Well, IFR means are you flying under instrument flight rules, flying when you can not see. I was a visual flight rule type pilot, not instrument rated. If I were to confess to him that I couldn't see where I was going, they'd probably put me in jail, hang me, and burn my airplane. Then they would sell my wife and kids, fine me and torture me.

I told myself I'd better not confess that I was possibly flying illegally, and I responded, "No, I don't think I'm IFR; I just can't see anything."

"Are you IFR?" he repeated. Well how can you know that your visibility is three miles if it is night and if there is nothing out there to see. How can you know if you can't see it? How do you know if it's not there, or if it is there?

I repeated, "No, I am not IFR, but I just can't see anything." As he repeatedly tried to get me to confess my plight, fear set in more. I said, "I'm going down, 8181 Kilo, I'm going down. I'm going to land this thing."

Louisville reappears...

He said, "You're breaking up, I can't hear you. Repeat. Repeat."

I descended 500 feet and was now a few hundred feet over the highway. Suddenly Louisville was put back on the earth. I realized I had flown into clouds. At low level I could see down but I couldn't see forward. As soon as I got out of the clouds and Louisville reappeared, I took a fresh breath. I said, "Cancel that last transmission, I'm going to fly on into Louisville."

With all the confidence that ignorance brings, I just continued my trip toward Louisville. Louisville disappeared again. Seconds later, the windshield was absolutely covered with buckets of water as I entered the most vigorous thunderstorm I'd ever seen in my life. Well, when you're in a car and you have rain, so much rain that you can't see where you're going, you simply pull over, stop, and wait it out. But you can't stop while you're up there in the airplane.

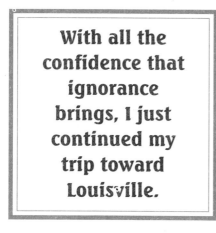

With all the confidence that ignorance brings, I just continued my trip toward Louisville.

I said to myself, "Self, you are tired, you are low on fuel, you are over the hills of Kentucky at night, your judgment is bad, you're getting ready to make a stupid mistake. Exercise your options while you still have some. Do not fly when you cannot see. Do not stall below 1000 feet. There are old pilots, there are bold pilots, but there are no old, bold pilots. Get out of here!"

I called on the radio again and I said, "I have to get out of this storm!" I turned around again, followed the old one minute turn rule and moments later I was out of the thunderstorm. Well, you see, in late afternoon in hot, humid August, thunderstorms are natural occurrences. I have learned that now, but I did not know it then.

I was heading away from Louisville, tired, low on fuel, I mean leaning on the pegs about now, and I said to myself, "Set this stinking thing down. Going down."

Flight service man calls back and he says, "8181 Kilo, what are your intentions? What are your intentions? You're breaking up; I can't hear you."

"Going down, going down." I kept saying "going down" as if I was going to crash.

After backtracking a couple of miles, I turned around, headed toward Louisville again, and decided to land in the westbound lanes of Interstate 64. I thought, "You know, the taillights on my airplane are not nearly as bright as the taillights on a car. How am I going to keep from getting run over?" As I was thinking about that, I was on final approach to this long, long interstate runway. All the bad things I ever did in my life seemed to flash before me in a few seconds.

"Going down, going down."

Depressing darkness...

Below me was an intense, scary, end-of-the-earth darkness, which became instantly, terribly depressing and I said, "This is awful! I mean it looks like a black hole. I mean there is nothing there; this is scary." As I continued my descent, the darkness became terribly dark and I said, "Something is wrong." I pushed on full throttle, yanked up the nose sharply into a very steep climb, narrowly missing a shadowy bridge across the highway.

I said, "Thank you, Lord. Yea though I walk through the valley of the shadow of death, I will fear no evil."

Bridges seldom come in pairs across an interstate highway in a rural setting; I decided that I would set it down immediately.

I thought about the taillights on the airplane again. I thought, "It would be my luck to do an absolutely beautiful landing on this long interstate runway and then somebody not even see me and run into me doing 70 miles per hour." What do I do? "Oh yes, I'll descend to about 10-15 feet above the highway, pass a car, and do 'S' curves in front of that car until I'm just real sure I've got the driver's attention. I will land in front of him and then pull off into the median and park and everybody will live happily ever after." Well that's exactly what I did: landed the plane, got out.

About the time I was crawling out of the airplane, the gentleman in the following car was at my door saying, "Are you alright?"

I said, "Fine."

He said, "You're lucky that I am a pilot. I knew the situation you were in and decided to drive in the middle of the road and block traffic for you. How would you like a ride into town?"

I said, "Thank you, sir!"

The Feds...

As we rode into town, I decided I'd better call the man at flight service because the last thing he heard from me was "Going down, going down." I called him and told him that I did actually land on the highway and assured him that I was safe. All he thought about was all those government regulations about reporting accidents and incidents and stuff like that.

I told the controller that I was safely down and that the bird was not bent.

Five times he asked me, "How's the airplane?"

Five times I said, "The airplane's fine."

"Is anything damaged? Anything bent? Anything destroyed? Anything bumped up, roughed up?" He was worried about filling out reports. I assured him everything was fine. In America, damaging an airplane, even if you own it, is a federal offense and there is a massive investigation. I was eventually cited for having a faulty right brake. They have to find something.

I hung up from him, called the state police, and said, "Hi, I'm Floyd Coates who just landed on your interstate highway and thought in case somebody reports it, you'll know whose plane it is." The dispatcher said he'd send an officer to talk to me.

I thought, "Huh? Here I have preserved my life, I've saved my airplane, and now I'm going to jail for committing the crime of landing on an interstate highway. Oh, well. At least jail will be dry and warm and on the ground."

Five minutes later a policeman drove up and he said, "Hi, are you the pilot?"

I said, "Yes sir, I am."

He said, "If the boss hears about your airplane on this highway, he'll make you dismantle it, put it on a truck and haul it away, but if we get out there quickly, you can fly it off." That sounded better than jail.

And of course by now, the thunderstorm had passed, the sky was clear. He drove me to the plane. The policeman turned on his spotlight

> **I've saved my airplane, and now I'm going to jail**

and shined it toward the sky to check for wires across the road, we crossed over the median, he blocked traffic for me and he said, "Take this thing off and get out of here.

Bowman Field is just a few miles ahead on your left and you can land there."

I said, "Thank you, sir." Oh, by the way, it turns out he was a commercial pilot. Isn't it nice to run into pilots who are car drivers, and pilots who are policemen?

I took this airplane off from one of the world's longest runways, Interstate 64 between Lexington and Louisville, Kentucky. I landed at Bowman Field in Louisville which had long runways and was well-lighted. Flying to my home base airport at Lamb, Indiana, which was a short, unlighted grass field, was not an option that night!

Going home...

I landed in Louisville, called my wife at home (she had gone to bed because she had to go to work the next day) and said, "Sandy, I have had a problem, pick me up at Bowman Field in Louisville." For the next hour, while she was driving to the airport to pick me up, I dreamed of sleeping all the way home. I was flat out tired, being up for nineteen hours.

Sandy did not like being disturbed from her sleep. When she saw me heading for the back seat, she said, "You drive...I am not interested." She promptly laid down on the back seat. I drove the silent hour home. We went to bed.

The next morning, Sandy went to work. The ladies in the office were all standing around a newspaper reading about some unidentified pilot who landed on a highway during a thunderstorm, waited it out, and then took off.

Who was he? Who was this mysterious pilot? Someone asked, "Sandy, your husband is a pilot, isn't he?"

She said, "Yes, and he was out flying last night, but he did not say anything to me."

What I learned...

That day God taught me an invaluable lesson. No story like this could be complete without learning something from it. What did I learn? Well I learned what my instructor had told me: There are old pilots, there are bold pilots, but there are no old, bold pilots. I learned not to fly when I can't see, especially when I'm not instrument rated. I learned that having fouled spark plugs in an airplane can cause you to go down, while fouled spark plugs in your car can just cause you to have slightly lower gas mileage. There are times when little things, like little sins, can foul you up badly or just be a minor inconvenience.

Pastor Robert Leach said, "Sometimes sin takes you deeper than you want to go and keeps you longer than you want to stay. Sometimes you get into situations where you really wish you could get out. Sometimes you get into situations, that as they develop, you ought to turn back, but you turn back too late." While going through life, watch out for the situations that seem to drag you in deeper and keep you longer than you should stay.

"Sometimes sin takes you deeper than you want to go and keeps you longer than you want to stay.

Most importantly, I learned that there are better resolutions to the problems of life than crash landing.

Since then, many things have changed. Rather than a radio that transmits on one of seven channels, I have two that transmit on seven hundred twenty channels

> **There are old pilots; there are bold pilots; but there are no old, bold pilots.**

each. So the controller can find me easily in the air, I now have a transponder. I now have four fuel tanks rather than two. I have GPS navigation system that locates me within feet rather than the old system that was usually accurate within miles. I have an exhaust gas temperature gauge that gives information to help prevent spark plug fouling. We now have radar that helps inform the pilot of the location of thunder storms. I then had one hundred hours flying experience; I now have a thousand. I have taken weeks of training to equip me to fly when I can't see.

New flying rules...

Nevertheless, most importantly, I have four more flying rules:

1. I do not fly if I do not feel good.
2. I do not fly if I think the airplane doesn't feel good.
3. I do not fly if the weather does not feel good.
4. No event is so important that I must go.

"Boy, the stuff you go through to take care of your customers!"

3

Middle of the Night Deliveries

The phone woke me at 12:30 a.m. It was Janet. She said, "Floyd, Fedders Air Conditioning Co. has changed their production line because of a rush order they received and they need some special knobs that we can make within the next few hours. Can you have them at their plant by 7:00 a.m.?"

The answer to the customer is yes...

"Of course, Janet. The answer to the customer is always 'Yes, sir!' If you have them here at my house by 4:30 a.m., I will have the knobs at their plant by 7:00 a.m. We will be waiting at their gate when they open."

A few months later, a similar situation occurred during dinner.

> ## The answer to the customer is always, "Yes, sir!"

We had guests for dinner and the phone rang. Again, it was Janet on the line and she said, "We have a customer that needs a rush delivery. They had a bad inventory and we have some parts in stock. Are you in a position to...?" I said, "Sure. I will meet you at the airport and tell him we will have the parts to his place within two hours."

Now, our company airplane is only a 1964 Cherokee four passenger with a 1,000 pound useful load. It only goes 150 mph, but it is very handy in making quick deliveries to distant customers in small towns and meeting their needs.

Our chief engineer, Jeff Hougland, has a similar aircraft. When there is a customer with a design problem, he is promptly at the customer's door. Even in very small cities with very small airports great distances away, we respond quickly. The customer doesn't think we are very far away.

A couple of years ago, my wife and I decided that we needed a one-week vacation. I said, "We've been flying commercially. Let's fly our plane. It will be fun." "But, while we're at it (and of course the most expensive words in the English language are, 'while we're at it'), let's visit a few customers on the way down to Florida." It was logical that we visit customers on a westerly route through Illinois, Arkansas and Alabama on the way down. We stopped to visit customers in Alabama, Georgia, South and North Carolina and Virginia on the route home.

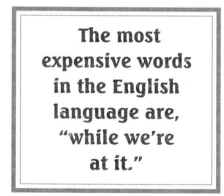

The most expensive words in the English language are, "while we're at it."

The last customer we were about to see was in Jacksonville, Florida. It was 1:15 p.m. The setting was a beautiful Florida day. My wife and I both visited with the customer on our annual visit. We told him how much we appreciated his good business and asked if there was any problem that we could help with. He responded, "Well, there is just one little thing. There is a quarter inch diameter hole in a part that you make for us that is undersized causing us assembly problems. We are contemplating sending those parts back to you for rework."

Solve the customer's problem now...

I knew that it would cost about $700 worth of freight each way to ship the parts to our factory. I realized that it was only about two days' work to rework the parts. I guessed that the defective condition had been developing over the last ten years and that the customer was just now realizing it. I suggested to the customer that Anne and I would be happy to delay the start of our vacation and rework the parts in his plant. That way, there would be no shipping of parts back and forth, reject notices, debit and credit memos, adverse reporting on vendor review for quality standards, etc. The customer instantly agreed.

He set us up in his warehouse with a drill press. Anne and I drilled parts on into the evening. We were able to get pizza delivered, so we took a fifteen minute break for supper and continued to unbox, unwrap, drill, wrap, box and restack parts until 12:45 the next morning. Realizing that we had just saved approximately $2,000 cost and had saved the customer significant inconvenience, we went to bed happy that night knowing that we had helped the customer.

The next morning, my wife was explaining to our friends why we were so late getting in that morning.

"You should have seen the expression on Floyd's face when the customer called his bluff about drilling the parts."

Well, honestly, it is true that I thought that the customer would say, "Well, just correct the problem the next time you produce them." We had a very pleasant, hard, long days' work reworking the customer's parts, and then enjoyed our vacation.

On a recent visit to that customer, he said, "When we have a new supplier who tells us how good his quality service is, I pull out of my top desk drawer one of those drills you used that night, Floyd, and I explain to him the standard for service that you set." I smiled and thanked him for his appreciation of us and again for his business.

4

Burglar in the Basement

In 1982, I won the Republican nomination for U.S. Congress from the Ninth District of Indiana. That year was a very busy year. One such day started at about 4 a.m. I showered and left home to speak to a Kiwanis Club in Connersville, Indiana, for their 7:30 a.m. breakfast meeting.

After that meeting, I visited with potential donors and campaign workers, traveling then to another city where I spoke at a luncheon meeting. Then I drove to Jasper, Indiana, roughly 220 miles away, for a dinner meeting with some political activists.

After that dinner meeting, I met with the leaders of the Republican Party in the after-meeting meeting. When that was over, I met with the core group of the real leaders of the Republican Party. Then I hung around to visit with the party boss, leaving Jasper well after midnight.

I made the long drive home, having been up and on the road now for some twenty-two hours. I dragged myself into my home. I almost couldn't make it through the living room to the bedroom. But, just as I was passing the stairwell, I heard what sounded like a burglar in the basement. I was so tired that I didn't even know if I had enough strength to make it to the bedroom. And if I made it to the bedroom, I would probably just fall asleep instantly and the burglar could just be free to take whatever he needed and leave. I didn't care.

But then the thought occurred to me, "No, probably what will happen is I will drag myself, exert every muscle I can to get to the bed and as soon as I get to bed, I'll be absolutely totally awake and wish I had thrown out the burglar."

I then stumbled down the stairs, trying to wake myself up, trying to gather enough physical and intellectual strength to handle a burglar confrontation.

The Burglar Identified...

But, as I approached the office in the basement, I heard the noise of a typewriter. As I drew closer, I found my twelve-year-old daughter typing. I said, "Beth, what are you doing?"

Not turning around, she said, "Don't bother me, Dad, I've got to finish these labels. We've got to get out this mailing for the campaign first thing in the morning." My eyes began to well up with deep appreciation for the dedication of this young lady, my daughter Beth, who cared enough to stay up all night if necessary to do what she felt was the right thing to do.

Her customer was her father, the candidate. Could I ask for better customer service?

5

Deer Like My
Woods Because I Put Salt in It

Have you ever noticed that kids like candy and people who give them candy because they like sweetness? Sweetness is an attractive chemical. I have occasionally been with people of whom it is said, "They could brighten up a room by leaving it." I have heard it said, "After I'm with that person, I feel like I need a bath."

I like to be around people that, after I've been with them for a while, I feel like I've had a bath. I like to be around people that, as soon as I see their faces, a smile comes to my face. That is my daughter, Sarah Graham. She is Sarah Sunshine.

Someone told me that if I poured 50 pounds of salt onto the ground in my back yard I would attract deer. I am now staring out the window and looking at three deer. If saltiness works with deer, I wonder if sweetness would work with people. I think I will try it.

I want to be the sort of person that people want to be with.

6

He Did Not Die Because I Tried

The right place at the right time

I guess few people have the opportunity to perform CPR on a fallen person. I had it twice. The first time I was at a watermelon picnic. The drummer in the band, a nearly 75-year-old man, suddenly keeled over. Though I was a candidate for Congress, shaking hands and kissing babies, I rushed through the crowd from the back of the outdoor amphitheater to the fallen man. I futilely attempted to resuscitate him until a local doctor pronounced him dead.

After that first experience with CPR my confidence was so shaken, I was reluctant to try again. Some months later, I had just arrived to check-in at the McCormick Hotel in Chicago. The lobby, crowded with about seventy-five people, was a little tight to get through.

I heard a scream. Somebody yelled, "Help, can anybody do CPR?" I figured that, with a large group of business executives, there should be at least a half dozen in the crowd who could, so I, who had just recently had open heart surgery, continued toward the check-in counter.

Who, me?!…

Twenty seconds later when the cry went out again for help, I figured, "If not me, who, and if not now, when?" Though tired, weak and with partially paralyzed legs, I pressed my way through the crowd to the fallen man.

Scene: Open elevator, large man, three hundred fifty pounds or more, face down on the floor. He was so large that I needed help to turn him over. I noticed that his pants were wet from having released his involuntary bladder muscle. I pressed my fingers against the side of his neck checking blood vessels and a pulse. Did someone else have an idea what to do? He was so large. I could not imagine being able to feel a pulse through all that fat, even if his heart had been beating full tilt.

> **"If not me, who, and if not now, when?"**

Then I beat him in the center of his chest, with what used to be the approved method for starting CPR. That produced no heartbeat either. I started pumping. Push, push, push with all my might, one thousand one, one thousand two, one thousand three, I couldn't remember how many thousands I was supposed to do. I figured I needed to circulate the blood first and then blow air into his lungs so the circulating blood would have some fresh air to get. It had been many years since Judy Wakefield had taught me CPR. I had forgotten whether I was supposed to do five pumps and three breaths, or three and fifteen, or two and one, I could not remember. All I knew was the guy looked dead to me. Here I was, tired, trying to save this huge guy's life.

After a few cycles I realized that the man was so large that when I would blow into his mouth I did little more than inflate his huge, puffy cheeks with air. Likely very little of my fresh air got down into his lungs. Probably none made it below the larynx. I thought, "Is this the time to follow the manual, which I couldn't remember anyway, or is it time to think?"

Air in...

I thought his lungs would hold five times as much as mine. What I needed to do was blow five deep breaths of my air into him rather than just one. I pinched his nose closed with my fingers, blew into his mouth, inhaled through my nose, blew into his mouth, inhaled again, blew into his mouth, inhaled again; blew into his mouth, inhaled again; blew into his mouth and inflated him. He then had a breath of fresh air. I quit inflating and resumed pumping. I breathed. I pumped. I breathed. I pumped.

Carrots out...

This went on for about ten minutes. From the hyperventilating I was doing to get air into him, I was beginning to feel somewhat nauseous myself. My wife knew how much I loved Snickers bars and how tempted I am to eat junk food while I drive. She prepared for me two pounds of raw carrots, cut into quarters, that I munched during my five-hour drive from Madison, Indiana, to Chicago. The half-digested carrots, eaten over that five-hour period, along with this tense situation and the hyperventilation, caused the carrots to slowly come up.

After several cycles of breathing into the man, I needed to clear my mouth and spit a few carrots onto the floor. I continued pumping, breathing, and spitting out a pile of carrots. After another minute or two, the pile of carrots being spit out became

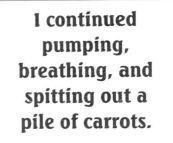

I continued pumping, breathing, and spitting out a pile of carrots.

even larger. As life was beginning to come into the man, all the people standing around thought they were his carrots, not dreaming they were mine. The humor of the situation did not occur to me until hours later.

I repeatedly checked for a pulse and could not find it on his neck. I continued breathing for the man and massaging his heart until the rescue squad came. At about the time they arrived, the man showed signs of life and being able to breathe on his own. I continued to pump and breathe just in case my diagnosis was wrong. I was relieved to learn the ambulance had come.

I live in a small town such that when an ambulance, fire truck or police car goes by, everyone in the house presses his nose against the window and looks out to see what's going on.

Slow to the rescue...

I expected the ambulance crew to come with sirens blaring, come to a screeching halt, kick down the front door, and to plow through the crowd.

I was not familiar with the ways of the big city. They were in no hurry to do their job. In fact, they very politely stood at the edge of the crowd making such statements as, "Pardon me, we are the paramedics, may we come through?" I inferred their thoughts of, " We have this cart to haul away the body and it would be convenient to us if you would step aside allowing us to pass."

I would have really been angered had the man not already been revived. He apparently did not need the rescue squad at this point.

The first tool used by the paramedics was interesting; it was a clipboard. The second tool to emerge was a pencil. "Can anybody give me the name of this man, address, phone number?" Obviously they wanted billing information.

I said, "Sir, I don't know who he is and I don't care. I want you to help him, save him, take him to the hospital."

The paramedic replied, "Please, someone help me turn him over and let's find his wallet and maybe we can find some identification." Knowing they were relentless, a few of us helped roll the man over so they could identify him. When they saw he was well enough to travel, they assisted him to the cart and wheeled him to the ambulance.

That night I was pleased to find a note in a nice large basket of fruit from the hotel manager thanking me for my work. I thanked him for the fruit.

Through the years, I have learned to trust God to arrange the situations—the right place at the right time. After God arranges it, it is my part to be the right person. Maybe that is why I had the opportunity to do CPR twice.

Now I know why they have annual reviews for CPR.

Each time – I tried. Each time – I gave it my best shot. If I had not been willing to be embarrassed because I walk with a limp, because I didn't use the perfect technique, because I did not know how they did CPR in Chicago, because I had a big stain on my shirt, because I am a Southern Indiana redneck...would he have lived? The things that tend to embarrass us usually bother us more than they bother other people. The guy who was dead that I pumped back to life did not care. I would bet he preferred my bad job to no job at all.

In being willing to risk embarrassment, we can sometimes achieve stuff that we might not otherwise. Sometimes there is no chance of compensation for all services provided. But what does that matter? It is more blessed to give than to receive. I had the pleasure of giving life that day.

7

I Learned from Jim Swanner

In 1967 I met Jim Swanner.

Between 1967 and 1969 I commuted three hours and forty-six minutes round trip to work each day. At Connersville, Indiana, there were four gas stations on the corner of Central and Third. Each morning I filled up the car at Swanner's Marathon. Jim's station had four sets of pumps, and there always seemed to be a line.

At one of the other stations I would see the proprietor busying himself reading the paper each morning at seven thirty. I once saw a customer at one of the other stations. I am sure they were open, but the customers all went to Jim's station. Why?

When I arrived, he would just start pumping, because he knew which formulation I used. Then he would greet me and start cleaning the windshield. If there was a stubborn spot, he would concentrate on it until it was gone. Sometimes he would knock on the glass, especially noticeable in cold weather. He would stick his head in to about where mine was usually positioned and glare carefully out the window to be sure that the window was clean from my point of view.

Every day he would pop the hood and check the oil level. He would pull out his gauge and check my tire pressures. He would ask me to turn on my lights to check bright and dim. He would check my brake and turn signals. He would check my washer fluid and brake fluid just on a routine fill up. He sold more air filters, oil, washer fluid, brake fluid, light bulbs and gasoline than the other three stations combined. Why?

Jim smiled.

Jim worried about his customers. That is why he had so many.

8

I learned from Jim Phagan

My neighbor, Jim Phagan, was extremely good, courteous, kind and helpful. If I were ever as good as he, I would let everybody know. I would be one arrogant dude. In life we need examples, heroes, role models, who set standards for us. Jim was one of these.

Jim was concerned that I not kill myself while doing a brake band replacement on my car. I explained to him that I was willing to do all of the work myself, but I just wanted him to watch to make sure that I got all of the springs and retainers properly positioned when installing the new brake bands.

After I was completely finished with the job, he noticed a spring lying on the floor. He asked humbly, "What's this?" Oh, of course he knew exactly what it was, but he wanted to take the sting out of my inability by presenting the improperly performed procedure gently. I reassembled the brakes with his extra guidance and gentle suggestion.

He was a furnace repairman. After completion of a middle of the night repair, on occasion he would realize that he was not comfortable with his repair. He would go back to the customer's house indicating he lost his screwdriver and wanted to go retrieve it. While there, he would correct his error. On his way out the door, he would flash the screwdriver that had been in his pocket all the time. Anything to help folks not feel uncomfortable.

Jim once came over and asked me if I was finished with his drill that I had borrowed six months before. He asked if he could borrow it. Now if you had borrowed something of mine six months before and had not returned it, I would really be angry. There was not a breath of that in Jim.

A gentleman, but not perfect...

Jim was not a perfect man, though.

One day I had trouble with the generator on my airplane. Knowing I could always depend on Jim to share my burdens and help me to learn and

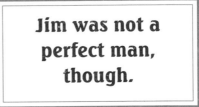

understand things, I jumped the fence and sought his counsel.

As we were walking through his yard, with the generator held on my shoulder, I suddenly vanished into the earth. He continued to walk, not noticing my absence until I howled for help. He then turned around and started laughing. He did not help. He called excitedly for all five of his kids to behold me.

Several years before city sewers came to that section of town, his home had been serviced by a septic tank. It had a quarter-inch thick steel plate over the top of it along with six inches of dirt. Over the years, the steel had rusted thin. It only needed me and my generator to break through.

The generator, of course, rolled through the lawn to safety. I was up to my shoulders in the aromatic contents of the septic tank. After the laughter subsided, he and his family pulled me out of the septic tank and hosed me off. Had it happened to someone else besides me, I would probably have laughed, too.

Jim was a good neighbor.

9

My Five-Year-Old Teacher

As you might know, little children are not my favorite things. In fact during the first two years of my own daughter's life, I played with her no more than ten hours. After she was two and out of diapers, I spent an average of two and a half hours per day working, playing, studying and traveling with Beth.

However, on one particular Sunday morning while my wife was in church playing the piano and singing songs, I could just tell from the aroma that this one-year-old child of mine needed a new diaper and needed it badly.

Previously, I had figured that if my wife was going to have a daughter that my wife could take care of the maintenance on her. But, being the good husband that I was, I figured changing one diaper in two years would not be too big of a sacrifice. I threw our daughter over my shoulder, grabbed the diaper bag, and carried our daughter like a sack of potatoes to the back Sunday school room.

Diaper change by the numbers...

I laid her out on the table and I said, "You are about to experience a diaper change." I figured it was a simple three-step process:

1. Remove the soiled diaper.
2. Clean off the mess.
3. Install a new diaper.

If I had a garden hose, I would have handled the clean up slightly differently than I did, but that proved to be unavailable.

After I laid her on the table and cleaned her up, I discovered my wife had this product called Pampers. To myself I said, "Self, all you have to do is do it. This is so simple any engineer could do it." I did it, stood the daughter up and the dumb diaper fell to the floor. I said, "Obviously there is something I missed."

After I put Beth back down on the table, an eighty-year-old lady appeared and said, "Floyd, I have lots of experience; do you want me to help?"

I responded, "Well, the mark of an intelligent person is the ability to recognize when he needs help and I do need help."

So she started fumbling around with the pamper and said, "What's this?"

I said, "That's a diaper."

She said, "That's not like any diaper I ever used. Mine were all three foot squares." She fumbled around for three or four minutes and was unsuccessful at attaching the diaper to Beth.

Diaper Desperation...

About that time, a five-year-old girl came into the room and said, "Pardon me, Brother Floyd, do you want me to change Beth's diaper? I change my brother's diapers all the time and I could do this for you."

The eighty-year-old lady and the engineer backed off and zap, zap, zap it was finished. And it stayed on.

> **"I change my brother's diapers all the time, could I do this for you?"**

What did I learn from that? Being a disciple means being a learner; one is never too old to learn. Furthermore, experience is quite a proficient teacher. Those with the apprenticeship are credentialed to teach others, even if they happen to be considerably younger. It behooves us to accept their ability to teach us. Never be too proud to be taught by the humble.

I am thankful for the no-charge service.

10

I Cussed Once; Soap Fixed It

Several years ago, I was officiating at the annual American Plastics Christmas dinner. We normally have introductions, speeches, food, and the presentation of Christmas bonuses and gifts to employees. While introducing my mother, Mildred Coates, I said, "And she is the only one who ever washed my mouth out with soap."

I was immediately embarrassed. I tried to save myself from embarrassment by asking, "How many of you have ever had your mouths washed out with soap?" Nearly half the crowd had moms like mine. I can remember well my mother wrestling me to the floor, taking this huge bar of Sweetheart brand soap, and wollering it around in my mouth. You have heard it said, "This hurts me more than it does you." I did not think it was true that day.

Mom's perfect cleansing...

Over the years, I believe I have cussed three times since 1954 and none of those times were within my mother's hearing. I fear a copy of this book will fall into her hands, and I will get my mouth washed out again, even though she's eighty-three years old. My mother is one of those who cared absolutely about the welfare and integrity of her children. She wanted to make sure our minds were clean, and if our mouths were not, she knew that was evidence of an unclean mind. Though the suds were in my mouth, the target was my heart. Every day Mom wanted to make sure the hearts of her children were in the right place. Mom knew it was her God-given responsibility to train up her children in the way she and God thought they ought to go.

I fear God and I fear my mom, so I guess the objectives of both of them have been satisfied. I am thankful for a loving God and a loving mom.

She was the supplier, and I was the customer. She knew what the customer needed and gave it to him whether he knew it or not. She gave even though the customer did not appreciate it at the time.

Part of customer service is giving the customer what he needs when he needs it. Another part of it is giving him high quality information to keep him from making a mistake. It is sometimes difficult to point out the customer is wrong and to do it tactfully, but it is better to be untactful than for the customer to waste a lot of time and money with a bad or troublesome part design. We have often heard that it's not good to shoot the bearer of bad news. Part of integrity and the expression of love of the customer is to warn them of unforeseen problems.

11

Ridiculous Rules

I own American Plastic Molding Corp. It has 130 employees. It is my intention and desire for it to be a good place to work. But, what is a good place to work? It must be safe, it must be decent, it must be pleasant, and it must be profitable. And, with those objectives in mind, we have established many guidelines for operation. Today, I'd like to focus on three of them.

One is, "Don't Cuss."

Good Cussing?...

Actually, cussing comes in basically two different types: there is bad cussing and good cussing. Now, before you judge me too harshly, let me explain. God did not command us not to say some four-letter words, but He did say clearly "Thou shalt not use the name of the Lord thy God in vain." Since He was very, very explicit in that one matter, I think that it is appropriate that we call it bad cussing. Therefore, at American Plastic, we have a rule. You don't do bad cussing. And, you also don't do good cussing.

You see, the good cussing often comes because of a person's frustration or irritation with another person. God made an explicit rule against the calling of other people by bad names. That is, you call no man a fool. We'll amplify that a bit. You don't call any man an idiot, a dumbhead, stupid and so on. In my early years in business, I committed that sin or made that mistake – whatever your theology is. But I know it was wrong.

So, we have a company policy against cussing. Good cussing and bad cussing – I don't want the folks in my employ saying bad things about God because I don't want Him to get angry at me or any of my folks. Secondly, I don't want to create anger, frustration or embarrassment to other people who work at American Plastic. So we do not allow personal cussing. We do not have personal cussing, the cussing against people. We do not have God-cussing, the improper and irreverent use of references to God.

The second is "Dress Modestly."

For Your Eyes Only...

I used to have a ridiculously tight rule called "long sleeve shirts, long pants." Everybody had to have almost every body part covered. Why? Well, it's simple. Sometimes some women feel it necessary to wear very loose-fitting tank top shirts that are too large except in the length, which is usually too short. They sometimes forget to wear undergarments and occasionally find themselves bending over to pick up something that was dropped in front of men in the factory. Sometimes women claim that it is too hot and what they really ought to do is get to wear less clothing so they can be cool.

I sometimes smartly remark that it's cooler in the shade. But the real purpose for the ridiculously modest dress code is that I want all of the wives of men who work in the factory to feel relatively confident that their husband's employer is doing all he can to minimize the temptation to those gentlemen to go astray.

Further, I would like the husbands and fathers of women who work at American Plastic to feel confident that the men at American are not in the habit of spending a lot of time looking over the bodily features displayed by women at American Plastic. I want them to feel comfortable having their loved ones work in this factory.

If we are going to have a good world, that good world must be inhabited by good people. One of the characteristics of good people is that they are loyal to their spouses and their families. It is my obligation to minimize the temptations whenever and wherever I can. I want American Plastic to be a good place for all people to work, a place where all employees and their families can feel comfortable and safe.

God rested, so will I...

The third is, "Do not work on Sunday."

Even God got tired. He rested. He determined that resting was good. There is enough stress in our lives that it should be relieved by a day of rest. Our company has worked two Sundays in thirty years. I intend that there be no more. I am not willing to pay the price for greater financial success if it includes working on Sunday. I do not expect the folks with whom I work to be pressured into working either.

12

What I Learned at Virginia Military Institute

Problem #1 – Your neighbor's house is on fire; what do you do?

Option #1 – Ignore. You can ignore it; you can watch it burn to the ground. You can say, "It's none of my business." You can say, "I don't care." You can say, "It's his problem." You can say, "There's nothing in the law that compels me to make his burning down house my problem; it is not my responsibility."

Option #2 – Judge. You can condemn him and say, "He should have been more careful and should have rewired his house and not stored gasoline inside his house."

Option #3 – Report. Tell the fire chief of your neighbor's negligence.

Option #4 – Restore. You can help put out the fire. And you can help your neighbor rebuild his home.

The Honor Code...

The first year of college, I went to Virginia Military Institute. They had a system of defining sin and minimizing its impact upon the corps of cadets. Since VMI was a secular, government-controlled institution, they didn't call it sin. They called it violation of the Honor Code. Lying, cheating, and stealing were not tolerated. They did not have many regulations in the Honor Code, but the ones they did have were enforced by the Honor Court, which judged student activity. If you were found guilty of lying, cheating, or stealing, you were gone. How did that happen?

The first day that I was at the military school, I got a lot of military orientation. At the last orientation of the day, they assembled us all in a large room and explained the honor system.

The honor system at VMI went something like this: you lie, cheat, or steal, you're gone. We don't want you.

> **The honor system at VMI went something like this: you lie, cheat, or steal, you're gone.**

One thing that you can expect out of VMI candidates, graduates, or cadets is that they don't lie, cheat and steal. They may not have their theology correct, but they don't lie, cheat and steal. Those characteristics were anticipatable from VMI cadets.

They had another rule: anybody who knows about someone that lies, cheats or steals is guilty of the same offense. Anyone who stayed after that moment agreed to abide by that code. Abide, of course, means that he would obey and follow it.

How did they enforce it? A student who saw another student violating the Honor Code reported him to a member of the Honor Court, a select group of twelve students. That student would say, "Cadet Joe stole some stuff yesterday."

The Honor Court had a meeting in the middle of the night. They did not have a public meeting. It was not conducted through the grapevine. Not everybody talked to everybody: "Did you see what Joe did? What do you think about...? Isn't it awful that...?" There was no whispering campaign. The system was simple: one cadet talked to a member of the Honor Court. The Honor Court met.

If the Honor Court agreed that Cadet Joe violated his honor and was guilty of violating the honor code of VMI, sometime in the middle of the night there was a ceremony.

They had a large drum, sounded like five feet in diameter. It made a huge, dull thud, which could be heard all over the barracks of a thousand cadets and woke up everybody. The night guard took a nightstick, policeman style, and banged on everybody's door providing a secondary announcement saying, "The Honor Court has met, the Honor Court has met, the Honor Court has met." With our bathrobes on, we went out to overlook the courtyard.

The ceremony went like this: "Cadet Joe cheated on an exam. He violated his honor. He is no longer worthy to be called a cadet. No cadet will ever mention the name of Honor Code violator Cadet Joe again for the rest of his life." The violator was then marched by the Honor Court out to a waiting taxicab. He, with his luggage, was put into the cab. He left VMI, never to return.

That was the VMI way – expel the offender with dishonor.

Obedience in Israel...

How did the children of Israel handle the problem? Numbers 15:32, "And while the children of Israel were in the wilderness, they found a man that had gathered sticks on the Sabbath day. And they found him gathering sticks and brought him unto Moses and Aaron and unto all of the congregation. And they put him in ward because it was not declared what should be done to him. And the Lord said unto Moses, 'The man shall surely be put to death.' And all of the congregation shall stone him with stones without the camp outside the gates. And all of the congregation brought him without the camp and stoned him with stones and he died as the Lord commanded Moses."

I think I understand English and what it said according to Numbers; the proper way was to uncover sin, judge it, and stone it to death. That's a little tough and quite a contrast from ignoring it.

Problem #2 – Your neighbor's soul is on fire – what should you do?

Option #1 – You ignore it. You may say that my neighbor's future is not my problem. It is rude to stick my nose into other people's business.

Option #2 – You condemn him.

Your neighbor has sinned. Your neighbor has stolen something. Your neighbor has lied. Your neighbor has cheated on an exam. Your neighbor has performed conduct unbecoming a Christian. Yet the man's soul is on fire, and what do we do? Can we close our eyes and say, "That's his problem?"

Option #3 – Report him to someone in authority.

Option #4 – You attempt to restore him.

Galatians 6 says, "Brethren, if a man be overtaken in a fault, (that is, if a classmate, a co-worker, or a neighbor lies, cheats or steals) you who are Christians restore such a person in the spirit of meekness, considering yourself lest you are also tempted. Bear ye one another's burdens and so fulfill the law of Christ."

Bear the burden of the sinner. That is, when my friend sins, that's my problem. When my neighbor's house is burning down, that's my problem. What he does about his burning down house is not my problem. What I do about his burning down house is my problem. What I do about my neighbor's sin is my problem. What he does about it is his problem, his responsibility...but I've got some obligation here, too.

> **When my neighbor's house is burning down, that's my problem.**

James said, "Confess your faults one to another, and pray one for another, that ye may be healed. The effectual fervent prayer of a righteous man availeth much."

I have a problem. I like to overeat. This is a problem that I need to be discussing with some of you skinny folks. You have self-control and I don't. James continued, "Brethren, if any of you do err from the truth (that is, you deviate from the will of God), and one convert him, let him know that that which converteth the sinner from the error of his way shall save a soul from death."

You saved your neighbor's house from burning down. Houses are a dime a dozen! Souls are expensive; you only have one of them and when you save one soul from death – eternal death, a fire of the soul – you have done an extremely good thing. You have a responsibility.

Matthew said, "Moreover if thy brother shall trespass against thee, go and tell him his fault between thee and him alone: if he shall hear thee, thou hast gained thy brother."

If I'm paying $10,000 to attend a school and somebody is stealing money from the school – raising the cost of operating the school – they're causing every student's tuition to be higher than it really should be. They sinned against everyone.

If I steal tools, merchandise, or supplies from my employer, it is a theft from the company that deprives customers of lower prices, other employees of pay increases, or stockholders of profits.

Restoration...

That's not the way God says to do it. Matthew says, go to him one on one. "I saw you cheat on an exam. I saw you steal the stuff. What you said to somebody the other day was not true." The brother has an opportunity to straighten the thing out. He has a responsibility to straighten it out. He is commanded by God to straighten it out.

"Moreover, if your brother trespass against thee, go and tell him his fault between thee and him alone. If he shall hear thee, thou has gained thy brother, pulled him from the fire. But, if he will not hear thee, then take with thee two or three witnesses that every word might be established."

Sometimes you theologians need to determine whether those are witnesses or whether they are judges, and what the role of witnesses should be. "And if he neglect to hear from them, tell it to the church. And if he neglect to hear from the church, let him be treated as a heathen. Verily I say unto you, whatsoever you bind on earth shall be bound in heaven and whatsoever you loose on earth shall be loosed in heaven. Again I say unto you, that if two of you shall agree on touching anything that they shall ask, it shall be done for them of my father which is in heaven." I'm thinking that's talking about unity and restoration.

Now, to review, I believe there are three possible approaches when a friend does wrong.

1. Ignore him.
2. Judge him.
3. Report him.
4. Restore him.

These Bible references, I think, refer to a sinning brother, his restoration, and his being pulled from the fire. I have done an inadequate and incomplete job of researching the area. I would love for somebody to take it on to themselves to finish this chapter and tell me what I should do.

I would like to know whether to ignore, judge, report or restore.

Would the world be better off if we did get involved? Would the individual be better off? How can we serve others better?

13

Dr. Hand Grenade

Grenade #244 – Chair in the Air...

As we all know on the graveyard shift, the most difficult time for most people to stay awake is around 5 a.m. One morning, I was on a 5 a.m. tour of American Plastic Molding Corporation and saw a man operating machine number nine. That machine, before the days of fancy and exhaustive guarding and safety equipment, had the potential of being able to do bodily harm on someone who was inattentive.

Of course, like most accidents, there is a chain of events that occurs – each one of which, if interrupted, could break the chain. One of the links in the chain is the man's motions of operating the machine which are repetitive, monotonous and sleep-inducing. When he can operate the machine with his eyes closed, he begins to be less aware of the dangers. I personally predicted that within ten minutes he would be the machine's victim.

I walked up to him, startling him by tapping him on the shoulder, and I asked kindly, "Could I borrow your chair a moment, please?"

He said, "Sure."

I then took his chair and threw it over my head. It landed twenty-five feet away and slid another twenty feet across the room. I yelled in his face like a drill sergeant, "If I ever see you sitting in a chair again the rest of your life, you are fired!"

> **Never be angry except on purpose.**

Of course, the rumors that followed had little correlation to what really happened. The sole purpose was to keep the man from killing himself. The occasional use of hand grenades is essential to wake people up – to make them aware of things they cannot see.

There is a rule: Never be angry except on purpose.

Grenade #658 – Have Nun Will Travel...

Another hand grenade I threw was in a meeting of the Manufacturer's Forum. The Scott County superintendent of schools was addressing the group with an incredibly long and boring dissertation on the fifteen-year plan for modification and improvement of our county's school system. This was in the wake of a public announcement that the public school had been de-certified by the accrediting association. In the midst of his speech, I, as a member of the audience, simply interrupted and said,

"Sir, I don't think you understand the gravity of the situation. In industry we have a practice of, if the customer has a problem, we solve it. And, we solve it now. We do not have fifteen-year plans – we have thirty-day plans. When General Motors decides that their car is going to be three inches shorter, that news affects hundreds of companies and thousands of employees and the transition is done in the thirty or sixty days that General Motors demands. We have no fifteen-year plans. With your fifteen-year plan, sir, there would be an entire generation of students to go by who would not have the benefit of adequate instruction. You shall have already retired well before your plan is put into effect. I perceive your plan is to promise long-term change and long-term goals so that you can avoid short-term responsibilities. I want to know exactly what it is you're gonna do this afternoon when you get back to your office to fix the problem."

> **"I want to know exactly what it is you're gonna do this afternoon when you get back to your office to fix the problem!"**

The problem is still not solved, but that superintendent of schools is no longer on the payroll. In discussion with folks after the meeting, I said, "We in industry sometimes do what's called subcontracting. That is, if we don't have time to do it, or we do not have enough of the proper skill, we place an order to do our work with some other supplier."

I explained that the local Catholic school sends about ninety-six percent of its graduates to college. All of the graduates from the Catholic school know how to read and write. I know that drugs, rebellion, disrespect, defacing of property are not problems at the Catholic school. Even though I am a non-Catholic, I do know the nuns understand education, discipline, respect, and most importantly, they care.

The key ingredients of education are: care for the students, knowledge on the part of the teacher and teaching skill, and a government that allows education to occur. Private schools as institutions allow teachers to care and teach.

My grenade went airborne. "Obviously our school system would be better off replacing the entire administration and staff, shutting down the local school, and leasing the property to a private results-oriented business which could hire and fire its own staff and its own teachers. There is a convent fifty miles down the road; we'll use a bus and bring the nuns in for teaching. We'll call it, 'Have Nun, Will Travel.'"

After the meeting, very few of my friends would talk to me, but I think we got their attention on the issue. Attention to the issue is usually the most important characteristic of the solution to the situation.

There is a rule: Never be angry except on purpose.

Grenade #121 – A Time to Leave...

After I became a Christian, I was introduced to an evangelical church wherein people acted as if they liked their God and their relationship to Him. I had been attending a mainline church. When the folks at that church discovered I had found a new church, the youth leader asked me to lead a youth group discussion on why the old, main-line church was a great church. In studying the materials from which I was to speak I was given the answers and my speech text follows:

"This church became great because it WAS evangelistic. It became a great church because it WAS a Christ-centered church. It became a great church because it WAS a loving church. It became great because it WAS an enthusiastic church. Because it WAS a lot of good things but does not now seem so, that is why I am leaving." I then left that church, never to return.

There is a rule: Speak the truth. Some need to hear it.

Grenade #999...

Grenade throwing does not have the objective of destroying everything in sight. It has the same general purpose of an agitator in the washing machine. Its purpose is not to clean, but to break loose the dirt and to bring to folks' attention that there might be a better way.

Sensitive to God's Spirit...

There are two animals, both in the horse family, which are used for transporting people. The first is a mule. If you want to get him to go to the left, you place your left foot on the left side of his neck and pull the left reign as hard as you can while hitting him on the right side of the head with a baseball bat. If you pull and hit hard enough, he may, if he wants to, change direction slightly to the left.

The other animal is a neck-reined horse. It has only to have its master's hand gently lay the reigns against the side of its neck. It responds as if it wants to do the master's will.

> **I often pray that I will be sensitive to the gentle leading of God's spirit.**

I do not want to be beaten to do the right thing.

I often pray that I will be sensitive to the gentle leading of God's spirit.

In these stories, the customers were almost unrecognizable. Let me list them: the sleepy employee, the superintendent of schools, the students, the taxpayers, and the apathetic church. None of them had a clue that they were customers. The customers are folks we serve. At the time of the events each, no doubt, felt that they were more victims than customers. I just wanted to help and serve them.

14

READY, SHOOT, AIM

We have all heard it said that there comes a time in every project when it's time to shoot the engineer and get into production. Sometimes we can put so much effort into planning that we never get around to doing the work. I remember as a child, reading a quotation: "Those who only plan are dreamers. They who only work are drudges. But those who plan their work are conquerors."

> **"Son, you would be a lot more effective in your work and in your speech making if you would read about the things you're talking about."**

Prone to act...

My father was an avid reader, reading about two hours per day throughout

all the years that I knew him. I, however, was more in-
clined to take action. Dad would always say to me, "Son,
you would be a lot more effective in your work and in
your speech making if you would read about the things
you're talking about."

I always thought of
telling him, "Dad, you
would be more effective
if you would stop read-
ing and start doing
something." However, I
never said those things
because I was always re-
spectful of my father
and I didn't believe it
was my role in life to tell
him what to do.

I do know that effec-
tiveness is more coupled
with activity than with
knowledge. Famous in-
ventor Thomas Edison
said, "Genius is one per-

> **I always thought of telling him, "Dad, you would be more effective if you would stop reading, and start doing something."**

cent inspiration and ninety-nine percent perspiration."

God said, "Faith without works is dead."

Often in doing a particular project, there is a need for
specialized information. With that need comes motivation to learn. When there is a need to know a particular
field of knowledge, the intensity of study in that area
increases sharply. At times, we're told to study things,
and we have no clue as to their relevance. As a result, the
study is sometimes shallow and superficial.

Prone to teach...

I often take people up for their first airplane ride. They are usually a little fearful. They do not know what to do, see, or touch. My approach is to immediately promote them to status of co-pilot and give them some responsibility. With that newfound responsibility, they suddenly feel they need to learn all they can in the next few minutes about airplanes, aerodynamics, airflow, engine operation, control surfaces, brakes, lights, valves, gauges, levers, handles, radios, knobs, fuses, straps, maps, microphones, headsets, etc.

We always start by walking around the airplane and pointing to the various parts, checking to see if they're all there and they wiggle like they should. We always check the gasoline and oil first to make sure we have enough, and I explain if we don't have enough gasoline and oil, the engine may not continue to run. In your car, you just coast to the side of the road when your engine seizes up. In the airplane, you have quite a different set of problems. So at this point, I go into a discussion of the things on the airplane that we inspect.

The inspection is so thorough that, by the time we finish with it, their comfort level has increased substantially. We climb into the cabin, then pull out the checklist. I usually call that the instruction sheet and jokingly say, "I read this once and, now that you're the co-pilot, it's your job to read this thing." As they read off each line, I am required to respond with "Yep" or "Check" or "Yes" or "Set" or "I always forget to do that" or "Crank" or "Start" or "Clear" or a litany of other such exchanges. At each item, if there's any question as to what the instrument or switch or device does, we get into a discussion. Then, the flying experience becomes much more of an introduction to a different way of life than just a ride in the sky. It becomes a learning experience.

Prone to build confidence...

I require the co-pilot to do most of the work. After all, the co-pilot has basically two jobs. The first is to fly the airplane and make everything happen under the supervision of the pilot. The second responsibility of the co-pilot is, if the co-pilot vomits and makes a mess in the airplane, the co-pilot has to clean it up. With this introduction, almost always, the newfound co-pilot always does a good job. After their first ride in an airplane, they truly have been a pilot.

My self-appointed job for virtually every younger person I meet is to try to cause them to have a lot more self-confidence, more knowledge, or to become more active. It is the lack of

> **I happen to think that most people can.**

self-confidence that prevents the young boy from introducing himself to the lady he would like to meet. It is the lack of self-confidence that causes people not to apply for the better job. The lack of self-confidence of most people causes them to say, "I can't, I can't, I can't." I happen to think that most people can. They just need a little confidence, success, knowledge, or motivation. It is my responsibility to help customers overcome fear and to have confidence to proceed with their projects or their lives.

After people fly with me for an hour, upon landing they usually tell their friends, "I flew it." I think that is a good gift.

15

Image and Value

Once upon a time, an owner of a restaurant whispered into the ear of one of the waitresses, "Please wear a larger smile and more makeup today."

She asked, "But why, sir?"

He responded, "The steaks are tough."

In the last few months, I have purchased raw steaks at the grocery for four dollars, eaten prepared steaks at Ponderosa costing eight dollars, and have been served elegantly delivered steaks for twenty-seven dollars.

The meat was the same, but in the first case, I had to cook it myself and do the dishes—but the price was four bucks. In the latter case, the steak was accompanied by dim light, soft music, and a waiter dressed in a tuxedo with a towel over his arm. This steak was delivered with ambiance.

In one case, the customer paid four dollars for the four-dollar steak; in another case, the customer paid twenty-seven dollars for a four-dollar steak.

It is our goal at American Plastic to give as much bang for the buck as we can. Not only do we want to deliver the best-molded part in the world, we want the customer to think we are delivering to him the best molded part in the world, too.

Not only do we want our service to be good, we want the customer to think it is good. We want our customers to think we are intelligent, sophisticated, aggressive, dynamic, energized people, and we want to be sophisticated, aggressive, dynamic and energized people. We want the customer to know that we care about him.

> **It is how you act when no one is looking that really defines character.**

It is our goal to be well paid for our services. I would not pay twenty-seven dollars for a steak if the waiter delivered it while wearing a tank top and jogging pants.

Show Respect...

The wearing of a necktie by gentlemen in the office creates the appearance that the customer is dealing with more sophisticated people. Now, granted, it is probably a little more comfortable to be wearing a flannel shirt, but that is not the image that American Plastics wishes to convey.

Why not dress up for our co-workers? Why should we dress up to look nice only when a customer is coming? When I get home, I wear my tie until my wife says take it off. I want to show my respect to her.

It is how you act when no one is looking that really defines character.

The more good things that are said by our customers, suppliers, employees, and former employees, the better our standard of living will be and the better our image will be in the market place.

Neat, clean, tight, orderly, proper grammar, correct – these are some characteristics of image.

But more importantly it is not the image we convey to our customers, but the image and attitude we convey to ourselves. Neatness and dressing-up is a way of showing our respect to each other.

We all know that K-Mart and Wal-Mart sell the same items that Macy, L.S. Ayres, and other high-priced department stores sell. We also know that the price is roughly half at K-Mart and Wal-Mart.

A few years ago, I toured a manufacturing plant in Switzerland and noticed that approximately two-thirds of the ladies who were working on an assembly line, were wearing dresses, and approximately fifteen percent of them were wearing high heels. By their dress and their neatness, they conveyed to me that they were making the world's most expensive, beautiful and exotic product, office chairs. Simply, we want to be distinguished as being the manufacturer of better parts.

Neat, clean, tight, orderly, proper grammar, correct – these are some characteristics of image.

16

Is He Famous or Is He Grandpa?

Our plans for dinner completed, we anticipated our visit with friends in this vacation paradise with delight. Stimulating conversation in elegant surroundings guaranteed a fine evening.

Our friends have two pre-teen sons, whose very existence threatened to disrupt our fun evening. These young men probably didn't need a babysitter, but definitely a referee! Our evening would be inconvenienced unless their mom found someone to stay with them.

We arrived at our friends' home just in time to hear, "Let's walk down to my in-laws' house; they're going to feed the boys and take them to the ball game." We breathed relief, realizing that our plans for the evening were safe. We walked through grass and down steep pavement hearing our friend chattering, "I can't wait for you to meet my in-laws!"

Mildly curious about her in-laws, we arrived at their front door. As we walked into their house, we saw Grandma supervising two boys eating dinner in front of the television. She greeted us warmly and welcomed us to their home.

In a far corner, Grandpa quickly rose to his surprising height to welcome us. As he approached to shake our hands, we thanked him for his willingness to baby-sit or referee the two boys and take them to their ball game!

> **Mr. and Mrs. George Beverly Shea made our evening possible.**

The boys grinned in relief when we moved from their view to another room to see Grandpa's newly ordered office. When our host showed us his tidy, computer-equipped room, we marveled less at the neatness than at the sixteen square feet of grills at our feet. As I crawled down the narrow steps to his basement, it was then I discovered that the grills were not for cold air. Rather they were for music from a vast number of pipes in his pipe organ in the basement. It was then that I realized in whose home we were visiting.

We left for dinner, bidding boys, and grandparents, good-by. Our happy astonishment grew as we realized that we were able to go out to dinner because two rowdy boys had the world famous gospel singer for Billy Graham as one of the referees for the evening. Mr. and Mrs. George Beverly Shea made our evening possible.

Great people are happy to help others and to serve. That is why they are great. And now you know the rest of the story.

17

Education of a Thinker

I haven't decided for sure whether higher education is a good thing. In my first week at Virginia Military Institute, I was given a fire hose that shot out a heavy stream of water at high pressure through a one-inch nozzle. I was given the job of cleaning a Jeep. Now, it wasn't just an ordinary mud-covered, filthy, dirty Jeep, it was the same Jeep that had been inside a garage all week long and was only taken out on Tuesdays and Fridays for the weekly parade. The parade just preceding the wash job was approximately one mile long through well-mown grass on a dry day.

You can't clean a jeep in five minutes...

The Jeep was truly covered with a very light film of dust. A heavy stream of water could, in the hands of a skillful person, completely remove all the dust from the surface in about a minute. Being inexperienced at cleaning Jeeps, I took about five minutes to do it, shut off the water and reported to the Sergeant saying, "Sir, Cadet Coates reporting one clean Jeep, sir!"

The Sergeant looked at me in a scowl and said, "A Jeep can not possibly be clean in five minutes."

I then thought, "Well, maybe I did miss something." I returned to the fire hose and sprayed down the Jeep for another ten minutes. I then reported, "Sir, Cadet Coates reporting Jeep is clean, sir."

The Sergeant said, "No Jeep can possibly be clean in ten minutes." It was then that I realized that my job was to hold a one-inch stream of water under high pressure in, on, or about the Jeep until I exhausted all of the time available. This way he would not have to be bothered with finding other meaningful work for me to do. At about the end of the time period, nearly an hour, I reported to him, "Sir, Cadet Coates reporting the Jeep is clean, sir!"

And he said, "Cadet Coates is dismissed." I returned to my room having fulfilled my military duty for that day. I began to chafe at the blatant waste of taxpayer's money. A chafing that remains today. Since 1983 I have been chairman of the Taxpayers' Watchdog Committee which exposes and opposes abuse of the taxpayer by government.

I was a bad rat...

A rat is what they call freshman cadets because they are treated by upper classmen as something very low. As a rat, it was my duty to memorize the menu every day. My wife says that my reasoning ability is nearly flawless, but my memory is terrible. Memorizing the menus did not happen to be one of my great skills. When enough upper classmen enough times discovered that I could not recite the day's menu, I was repeatedly sent to the rat disciplinary committee which always found me guilty.

For nearly a semester, I found myself walking penalty tours on Wednesdays and Saturdays for a period of five hours per week. I was confined to the barracks all other times that I didn't have military duty. This didn't do anything to help my memory, but it did help me to realize the basic stupidity of some of the activities of an educational system. I will confess that, a few months later, somebody did point out to me that if I would memorize the entire week's menu one time, it would have been suitable for the whole year, since it never changed.

I wish I had learned that earlier.

18

How To Keep
Customers Coming Back

More Restaurants...

Edgar Sumale, the head waiter of the Santa Fe Mexican Restaurant in Scottsburg, Indiana, always asks if I would like a chocolate Pepsi as I am walking into his restaurant. He knows that my wife, Anne, wants "water-no-ice." His English is difficult to understand, but his customer service is good. Tammy Robinson at the White cottage does the same thing. At Best Western, Terri Hayes always gets me a Pepsi, no ice, without asking. We do not eat at these restaurants because the food is better or cheaper. We eat there because we are made to feel that the waiters care about us.

While in Denver a few years ago, I finally learned what a waiter is. A waiter is someone who stands beside your table, dressed in a tuxedo with a towel draped over his bent forearm and he waits there to refill your glass after each sip of water or to wait on any of your other needs. It is certainly tempting to go back to the restaurant where the waiter made me feel he cared about me.

Engineers:

Sometimes engineers in the development of a product can make it user friendly. Even though they may never see the customer, they can help serve the customer by making the product easier, safer, more comfortable, more foolproof, less expensive, lighter, or more durable.

Gas stations have gone to swipe the credit card yourself, pump the gas yourself, no lines and save money. You might think this is not customer service, but it is an improvement on waiting in long lines at the cash register.

Gas station owners have learned that the customer is willing to pay double for a Pepsi or a gallon of milk just to avoid the hassle of a grocery.

Repairmen...

Have you ever had a water leak, an electrical problem, a roof leak, a drywall repair, a painting project, any project that would take less than two weeks to do? There are two aspects of the problem. One is, it seems nearly impossible to get a contractor to come and look at a small job, then when he says he will do it, it seems that he simply takes my job and puts it in his deep file of things he ought to do sometime. He tends to not return phone calls and not show up when he says he will. Sometimes I take off work to meet him at a particular time to show the job to him or to be here while he is doing the job and then he doesn't show up. I have often thought that a serviceman who did what he said he would do, when he said he would do it, would be a pearl of great price. I have often thought that a good, reliable service man could make a very good living.

I recently had a leaky roof. Over a period of three months, I called several people. Two looked at the job. Only one of them acted the least bit interested in doing it. The contract for the repair did not go to the best bidder, it went to the only bidder. What an enviable position as a supplier.

I do not know whether his work was good or bad, whether his price was high or low. But, if I need another repair, I will call him because he showed up.

Department Store

I went to Wal-Mart, not knowing where a particular item was. After a few minutes, I was able to find a sales clerk and asked specifically, "Do you know where a particular item is?"

The response, "Yes, I will be happy to show you." After that item was found, the clerk responded, "May I help you find anything else?" That clerk made my shopping almost a pleasant experience.

The Aircraft Mechanic

While in a distant city, I had a burned out thermo-couple on the exhaust gas temperature gauge of my airplane. While the mechanic was working, he noticed a missing bolt in the exhaust system and replaced it without further instruction from me. I am happy he cared enough about his customer to do a little more, on his own initiative.

> **I am happy he cared enough about his customer to do a little more, on his own initiative.**

What Are the Characteristics of Good Customer Service?

▲ He makes deliberate effort to deliver the best possible product, consistent with the terms of the agreement.

▲ He makes every effort to reveal any problems to the customer.

▲ He carries his concern for the customer's success in the use of his product by being sure it is suitable for the use intended.

▲ He carefully reviews the specifications to discover any errors or omissions that might cause the customer a problem even though those problems may not affect him, the supplier, at all.

▲ He promptly delivers product and returns telephone calls promptly, returns documents promptly.

▲ He tells the truth.

▲ He does not over-promise.

▲ He is not deceptive, either actively or passively, in any of his language and speech.

▲ He gives honest measure, honest count.

▲ He creates, justifiably, a feeling of trust and confidence on the part of the customer.

Knowledge. A thorough knowledge of your product or service can save the customer from over or under buying and specifying. Your knowledge of materials, processes, products, and intended use by the customer greatly enhances the value of your product or service. Additional learning by you can reduce friction and tension by the more appropriate selection of more precise words that more nearly convey the intended thought.

19

"Our Toilets Are Not For Customers"

It was a Saturday in November of 1974. Our home had been blown over by a tornado a few months before. We were in the market for light fixtures for our new house. We needed to equip it with lights for the porch, lights for the trees, lights for the garden and the fountain, lights for the garage, Christmas lights, basement lights, dining room lights, star lights, lights for the everything. We selected a lighting store in Jeffersonville, Indiana, as the most likely store from which to buy all these fixtures. After we had been in the store for 30 minutes, we had written a list of $1,700 worth of light fixtures that we intended to purchase. That was about half of what we intended to order.

I suddenly felt nature's urge and I asked the sales lady, "Pardon me, ma'am, do you have a bathroom?"

She responded,

"Our Toilets are Not for Customers!

"However, if you get into your car and drive south a couple of blocks then turn east and go another block or so, you may find a restaurant which will let you use their toilet."

I thought about that and realized that I was going to have to interrupt the writing of the order for $3,000 worth of light fixtures. I was going to have to interrupt it to find some other business in town whose toilets were for customers. As I got into my car, I realized that I should probably place my order with someone who was more concerned with my needs. Some twenty

years later, I did go back. They now have, in this multi-million dollar store, toilets for their customers. I like it when people learn to see things from the customer's point of view.

20

K-Mart Tales
and Customer Service

K-Mart Tale 1...

I was in K-Mart. I had selected three items for purchase. Approaching the front of the store, I came to nine cash registers. As always, there was one layaway clerk, two cash register attendants, and absolutely no one at the other seven checkout stations.

My best estimate told me it would take about fifteen minutes to get from the end of the line to the register area. Spying the layaway section and realizing I did not need my three items right away, I headed to layaway. I said to the clerk, "May I lay away these items?"

Even though she was surprised that I would layaway only fifteen dollars worth of items, she began to fill out the layaway forms. After I signed my portion and she signed hers: I made a down payment of three dollars.

Then I asked, "Is this properly laid away?" After she confirmed that the layaway process was complete, I then said, "Could you explain to me what I need to do to take my stuff out of layaway?"

She replied, "You must bring this receipt and give me the other twelve dollars."

I laid out twelve dollars and said, "I want my stuff."

Surprised, she said, "What?"

I answered, "As soon as you take this twelve dollars, I will leave. If I had waited in the other lines, I would still have six people in front of me."

She said, "Why didn't you just tell me? I would have treated you like a normal customer."

I said, "But your sign says, for layaway and returns only."

K-mart Tale 2...

One day I needed an oil filter for my car, and with Beth's birthday party only minutes away, I was in a hurry. I ran into K-Mart. Frustration set-in. It seemed that at K-Mart if you need help, there is absolutely no one available to help you find what you want.

> **Having clerks around to help you would defeat their plan to relieve you of as much cash as possible.**

Now if you know the store, you also know where to find what you want. If you don't know the store, you'll find that K-marts are designed to be browsed and not designed for you to quickly find what you want. If the customer has to look harder to find what he wants, he will browse more and buy more than he intended. Having clerks around to help you would defeat their plan to relieve you of as much cash as possible.

So, I took my cart and walked up all the aisles, looking everywhere for a clerk. Finally, I said to myself, "There is always a sales clerk in the electronics area." There were no clerks in electronics. Then, I noticed a telephone and said to myself, "I will go to the phone, look up the phone number of this store (and no doubt it will have more than one line), and I will dial K-mart."

I looked up the number, picked up the handset, and did not get a dial tone. I pushed one of the buttons on the top and it did nothing, the next, nothing, the next, dead, next...next...next. But then, the tenth button. I still did not get a line but when I pressed it, there became a silence and I could hear myself breathing all over the store.

Realizing that I had tapped into the store's paging system, I said in an authoritative voice, "Attention, attention! Customer desperately needs help in electronics." I hung up the phone. Music came back on. I walked out in the aisle. Two young girls came running down the aisle. To the first one I said, "You get a kite and a ball of string for my kid." To the second one I said, "You get an oil filter for my car." It took some creative effort, but I became a happy customer.

K-mart Tale 3...

Once upon a time, I was driving down the road and—I'm sure none of you have ever had this problem—I had a digestive problem. I figured the only remedy was to go into K-mart and buy myself a new set of underwear. So, I parked my car in the emergency parking spot in the front and went in. I figured that if ever anyone had an emergency, I did. I walked into the center of the store. I could not find the underwear rack anywhere. So, I cupped my hands and yelled as if I were atop a high mountain and said, "Helloooooooo. Customer needs help. Is there a sales clerk heeeeeere?" I waited for the sales clerk to come.

Moments later, a woman walked slowly toward me and said, "May I help you, sir?"

I said, "I need a set of underwear, size thirty-eight, and I need it badly." She pointed over two counters. I glanced over, and I saw what seemed like acres of whiteness. There were pillows, blankets, tablecloths, t-shirts, under-wear, over-wear, sheets. More white things than I ever imagined. I figured that if I ever got to it and found my size, a major disaster shall have already occurred. I said, "You don't seem to understand, I need some underwear, and I need it now."

She responded, "I'm sorry, sir, that is not my department." After a few moments of insistent explanation, I was able to persuade her to help me.

> **"I'm sorry, sir, that is not my department."**

K-mart Tale Summary...

There is a reason why I include these K-Mart tales. Believe it or not, my intention is not to belittle a merchant—even a mega-merchant like K-Mart; nor is it my intention to belittle the people who work there. Rather, I want to communicate a lesson. I know what it feels like to be a customer—a customer who doesn't know all the answers and customs of the place; a customer who is in a hurry for valid reasons; a customer who has a real emergency.

There are real people with real problems who walk through our doors every day. Some may even have problems and needs greater than sacred company policies. They do not come seeking corporate service. They come seeking personal service.

21

YOU'VE GOT TO LISTEN TO THE CUSTOMER

Listen...

Arby's has unquestionably the best roast beef sand-wich in the whole world. A few years ago, my wife and I went to an Arby's drive-through. Of course, the reason you go to a drive-through is so you don't have to get out of the car, so you can get what you ordered quickly and get back on the road. We took our appropriate place in line at an Arby's drive-thru and placed our order. It was a relatively simple order. In total, it was one Arby-Q sandwich, one Roast Beef and cheese with horsey sauce, and ketchup, napkins, and two large waters.

Now, on the surface, that does not seem to be too diffi-cult. We then proceeded to the pickup window. The cost was announced, and I paid it. I was then handed a sack and received the signal that I was free to leave.

Listen again

I decided, before I drove off, to put the car in park and unload the sack. I immediately noticed the two waters missing. So I knocked on the window with no response. I then knocked on the window again and asked for the two waters. They were politely and quickly delivered. I set the two waters on the dash.

I continued to unload the sack, locating the two sandwiches. Then I saw, while unwrapping, neither sandwich had any condiment installed on it. I placed the water and sandwiches on the dash for easy viewing. I then knocked on the window again and said, "Hi. I ordered an Arby Q and a Roast Beef and cheese, Horsey sauce and ketchup and there's nothing on my sandwich. Could you give me some Horsey sauce and ketchup, please?" The salesman then handed me some packets. Among the packets was mustard and Horsey sauce, which I carefully laid out on the dash of the car.

Listen again...

I took inventory again and realized that I was still short of ketchup. I knocked on the window again and said, "Sir, I ordered an Arby Q sandwich and a Roast Beef and cheese with Horsey sauce and ketchup and you gave me an Arby Q sandwich and a Roast Beef and cheese sandwich as I ordered, but you didn't give me the Horsey sauce and ketchup that I asked for. When I explained the problem earlier, you gave me horsey sauce and mustard so I gave you back the unneeded mustard, but you forgot to give me the ketchup. Could I have some ketchup as I ordered?"

He turned around and reached into a bin and got a handful of ketchup packets. Well, I then took those ketchup packets and laid them out on the dash of the car

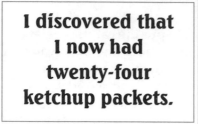

I discovered that I now had twenty-four ketchup packets.

to be sure that what I got was really ketchup.

Laying them out on the dash, I discovered that I now had twenty-four ketchup packets thus twenty-two more than I needed and three more mustards. I knocked on the window again. This time he refused to come back to the window. I kept knocking. The manager finally came to the window and said, "May I help you, sir?"

I said, "Yes sir, I think you can. A little while ago, I ordered an Arby Q sandwich and a Roast Beef with cheese, Horsey sauce, ketchup, napkins and two waters. What I received was almost everything I had ordered except the Horsey sauce and ketchup, and he gave me mustard which I did not want. When I explained that to the other gentleman, he took back the unneeded mustard and gave me twenty-two ketchup packets too many and three more mustards that I do not want. So, I would like for you to have these back because we don't have any use for them in our car because we're traveling."

The manager then received the ketchup and mustard packets back. I thanked him, then I reviewed the arrangement of my order on the dash, and I found that I had the Arby Q sandwich and the Roast Beef sandwich with cheese. I now had horsey sauce, ketchup, and two waters, but they hadn't given me the napkins that I requested.

Listen again...

I knocked on the window one more time and I said, "Pardon me, sir. I appreciate your help in straightening out my order, and all of the food is now correct, and I received my two waters, and I have returned all the stuff I did not order and do not want, but could I trouble you for the napkins that I requested when I placed my order?" He gave me a stack of napkins two inches high. By now the sandwiches were nearly cold, but the order was now correct.

Through this, I learned that it is better that you listen to the customer. Things go a lot better if you hear and respond to his needs. Giving him what you want to give him may not result in a satisfied customer. Giving him what he did not order may frustrate him and unnecessarily consume his time and yours and all the customers behind him. This may cause you to be too busy to take someone else's order.

I learned that there is never time enough to do things right but always time enough to do them over.

> **I learned that there is never time enough to do things right but always time enough to do them over.**

22

"Major on the Majors...
Productivity of the Church"

Once upon a time, I tried to persuade a church pastor what he should do with his time. I asked him, "What is the most important thing to you? Why do you exist?"

He said, "Well, I preside over the church."

"Why does your church exist?" I countered. He fumbled around and couldn't come up with a really good answer. Then I proffered an idea. I suggested that his job was to persuade people to become Christians. His church, with a $50,000 per year annual budget, in a three-year period, gained one convert. That means to me, that the average convert cost $150,000.

Cost Reduction...

I suggested to him that he go on a commission basis and that I would pay him $500 per convert; that way he could focus his attention on recruiting and getting people saved. He summarily and instantaneously rejected the idea, saying, "That's putting a price on a soul." I agreed with him that souls were worth the $500 each to me but were costing the church $150,000.

He continued to spend $150,000 per soul, and he also continued to cut the grass, rake the leaves and do the maintenance at the church in almost total disregard for soul-winning evangelization and discipleship.

Still feeling this a good idea of offering $500 per convert, I then contacted evangelists. I figured that this was a great way to spend some of God's money. I asked evangelists how many they had gotten saved in the last year. Many answers ran from tens to hundreds. I said, "Wait a minute."

"I'm not interested in warm-overs and revived. I'm talking about people who have never been exposed to the Gospel before, have not known anything to speak of about God. You introduce them to Christ and, after a 6 month period, they give evidence of being Christians. (That is, kind of like ducks. If they walk like ducks, talk like ducks and lay duck eggs, they're probably ducks). The characteristics of a Christian are: they probably come to church, they probably study their scripture, they probably contribute to the welfare of the church, and they're probably interested in getting other converts as well."

Put your money where your mouth is...

Many pastors and evangelists turned me down as being a mercenary. Then one finally said, "It's a good plan, Floyd. Let me see what I can do." He then changed the focus of his ministry from managing the church to developing new Christians. About a year later, he sent me an invoice for $4,500.

I called him and said, "Hey, what's this all about?"

He said, "Well, I have nine converts that fall into the definition that you laid out. They walk like ducks, talk

like ducks and lay duck
eggs. You offered $500
per convert . . . so pay
your bill."

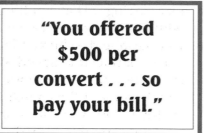

"You offered
$500 per
convert . . . so
pay your bill."

I congratulated him
on refocusing his minis-
try. I said, "OK, I'll pay
it, but I need an easy
payment plan." I made
an immediate $2,000 payment and another payment of
$2,500 a few weeks later. His strategy as a pastor was per-
manently changed. If you major on the majors, the mi-
nors will usually resolve themselves.

The customers in this case were the parishioners of his
church. They, as an evangelical church, had been experiencing stagnation until a change occurred in the values of
the pastor. When the pastor changed what was important to him (the recruiting of converts rather than cutting
of the grass on the church lawn), his customers received
more bang for their bucks.

23

What I Wish I Had Learned at Hanover College

I attended Hanover College and received a Bachelor's Degree in Physics in 1967.

One of the first confrontations I had with a Hanover College professor was in the theology department. As a Christian who takes seriously his relationship to God and his responsibilities, I was looking forward to studying theology. What I didn't realize was one of the most popular theological philosophies floating around at the time of my Hanover experience was being propounded by a particular instructor.

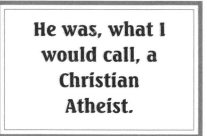

He was, what I would call, a Christian Atheist.

He was, what I would call, a Christian Atheist. That is to say that he had the theological training of someone who had studied the great theological thinkers, he just did not happen to have taken much time to study the scripture as given by God.

Problem with theology...

We were assigned to read two Bible passages in our first day in his class. He directed the discussion the next day. He said, "Did anybody notice conflicts in the two presentations of an event by two different people?" He then explained, since the Bible is self-contradictory, it should be dismissed. What he failed to understand is a basic law of witnesses and evidence. That is, an event really did occur, although two slightly different accounts given by two different people, who saw the event from two different vantage points, differ in minor matters of detail. The fact that they do differ really adds substantiation to the claim that there was a miraculous feeding of 5,000 men. He summarily denied this miracle of Christ. The fact that the accounts are different means that there was no particular conspiracy to correlate fabricated stories, thus increasing the probability of the event really having occurred.

It was at Hanover College where I was taught that the most plausible explanation of the virgin birth of Christ was that the Virgin Mary probably had a premarital sexual relationship with a Roman soldier.

After a few days in his class, the professor seemed to recognize the fact that I was chafing. He asked me to stay in after class and chat with him. He asked me what was wrong, and I told him that I thought his class was too pornographic. Well, I didn't know then what pornographic meant, but what I witnessed, of course, was not pornography but rather atheism and secularism being promoted as theological understanding.

He asked what church I attended, and I told him that I attended the Nazarene church. He said, "Oh, I understand. Let's have this arrangement: you come to class every day, don't read any of the subject matter, don't take any of the exams, keep your mouth shut and I will pass you.

> **"Keep your mouth shut and I will pass you. If you open your mouth, I will flunk you."**

If you open your mouth, I will flunk you." Understanding this man stood between me and graduation, I figured it would be wise for me to comply and keep my mouth shut. He kept his word. He gave me a D minus in theology.

Problem with geology...

My next encounter was with the geology department. Now, some of us believe, based on our religious principles and not disputed by scientific evidence otherwise, that God created the world in six days and rested on the seventh. Some people of a secular and humanistic philosophy expressed their values by denying the existence of God. Their religion is based on a big bang. And from that "nothing" in the bang became "something" in which one chemical becomes another and another and another and another. This, of course, violates most of the basic laws of thermodynamics and physics. They feel that if they can prove that God is not needed for our existence, then we need not be subject to His laws. The theology and geology departments worked those issues in a well-coordinated fashion.

> **"So, we are now going to study how the world got here without the help of God."**

In the first day of the geology class, he said, "During this course we are going to study the origins of what we see around us. There are two theories: one is of creation and one of evolution. Of course, no thinking person could possibly believe that all of this complexity was created. Therefore, we will study how it really happened." As if to say, "So, we are now going to study how the world got here without the help of God."

Problem with economics...

At Hanover, they taught me that you could not legislate morality. That was a cute phrase which provided some excuse for giving license to improper conduct. Government has determined that the teaching of Christian moral values is improper, while the teaching of atheistic, Marxist, immoral values is proper. The result in high school shootings is not surprising. Government formerly forbade abortion; now over one-fourth of children are killed before birth. Government discourages the maintenance of the traditional family by its higher tax on married couples. Government encourages immorality of its citizens by making the tax code some twenty-three and one half feet thick. How can anyone understand it? How can anyone comply? Government destroys individual responsibility by its high taxation and statements that it will perform people's moral responsibilities. Government rewards unproductive companies and individuals at the expense of the productive. Government protects and houses the convicted at the expense of the injured. Maybe government does not legislate morality, but it sure does encourage, license, make immorality more profitable and convenient.

At Hanover College, I soon began to realize that some of the professors knew their subject matter and enjoyed helping students to learn it. Then, there was another group of professors who really didn't care. In fact, the bad professors, to hold attendance up in their classes, always took attendance. The good professors didn't have to take attendance. Even if the students were sick, they would go to hear the classes. Those classes were good, interesting, relevant, important and were delivered by teachers who cared. You see, some professors thought it was their job just to give lectures, while some professors thought it was their responsibility to cause the students to learn.

Problem with the dean...

Recognizing this problem, I went to the academic dean. I explained, and he asked me the question, "What percentage of the teachers are good and what percentage do you think are bad?"

I responded, "I think one-third of them are good, and I think two-thirds are an absolute waste of my time and my money."

He rubbed his chin and said, "Yes, that's about right."

Well, I thought about that a while, and I said, "Wait a minute. In my life, am I willing that a third of the loaves of bread that I purchase have bread in them, a third of the cereal boxes that I purchase have cereal in them? Would I be content that a third of the new cars that I buy would have engines in them?"

> # If the college had known that two-thirds of its product was worthless, it should be sued for malpractice.

Nevertheless, he seemed to be happy to accept a third as "That's about right, which is okay. What's wrong with you, Floyd?"

Problem with quality...

Colleges need to realize they are businesses selling a product called education. Quality control procedures need to be put into place to measure the effectiveness, efficiency and quality of the delivery system and the end product.

I, along with all the other graduates of Hanover, was cheated. I got about a third of what I paid for at Hanover College. Someone suggested that if the college had known that two-thirds of its product was worthless, it should be sued for malpractice. A doctor or manufacturer certainly would be.

24

Lies, Fraud, and Deception

I wish this chapter were about somebody else, but it is about me.

The background of this story is 1974, during the Arab oil embargo. In the United States, there were shortages of everything petroleum-related. And, of course, a plastic material, commonly called ABS, was in short supply. In times of raw material shortage, suppliers would sell their raw materials to their long-standing customers first. If there were a shortage, the new customers would be the last in line. I was at the end of the line

The day came, parts were due, and there was no raw material from which to make the parts. Now, the parts were a non-critical application relating to physical characteristics, but indeed the formulation specified by the customer was very specific. The supplier did not have any of that raw material, but he could sell me something that was very similar in its properties. He did.

The deception...

I went ahead and made the parts out of the similar, as good as, but definitely wrong material. Upon shipping the parts, I was called upon to write a statement certifying that I had made these parts from one material when indeed, I had made them from another.

A few weeks went by, and I knew that I had done wrong. No excuses, just wrong. Even though there was no intent to defraud the customer, I had in fact had to pay more money for that raw material than I had been paying for the correct material. It was wrong. I needed to call the customer and make restitution.

The confession...

So I called the customer, and I said, "Joe, Floyd Coates here. I have a problem. I have done an incredibly stupid, selfish, damaging thing, and I want to do whatever it takes to make it right." I explained to him what I did, and I explained to him that he had ten thousand of my ten cent parts that went into about three hundred thousand dollars worth of his product that did not comply with the specifications.

I said, "Joe, I know what I did was wrong. I do not have, at this time, financial strength to pay for all the damages that I may have done to your company. I hereby confess to what I have done, and I will do anything that I can to make right what I did wrong. And, if it takes working for five years to earn enough money to pay you back the cost of rectifying what I did, that I will do."

Joe responded, "I don't believe this. I really don't believe it."

And I said, "Again, I say I am sorry, Joe. It is bad and all I can do is ask you what can I do to make it right."

He responded, "No, I'm not talking about that. I am saying that I know that people lie on certifications all the time, but I have never had anyone call and tell me that they did."

The change...

After that I decided that I would never lie any more on certifications.

> **"Again, I say I am sorry, Joe. It is bad and all I can do is ask you what can I do to make it right."**

I had another customer who repeatedly asked for certifications on their parts. That customer designed a battery carrier that I produced. All was fine until he redesigned his battery to be slightly smaller. He wanted to continue to use the part produced by me for this new battery. The problem was that the battery would slip out of the carrier. I repeatedly told the customer that his mold needed to be modified to make the part smaller to his new specification. He did not want to spend the cash to make the correction, however, and refused to have the mold changed.

I wrote certifications as he requested, but they all had the added statement "all of the dimensions of the part were not to specification." It was kind of a non-certification certification.

When a battery slipped out of a carrier breaking the foot of his consumer, my customer had to admit in court that he knew the product was bad because every shipment of parts I made I told him so.

Telling the truth is often painful, but it is better in the end. I can sleep better at night, too.

25

THE CASE OF THE MISSING CHRISTMAS CARDS

As an eight-year-old child, I lived in Rochester, New York. Each day, while walking home, I noticed a mailbox in front of a large house. The folks who lived there were seemingly better off than we were. One day, on the way home from school, I decided that I should find out what kind of mail they received. In opening their mailbox, I discovered that they had a package. I wondered what was in the package. I looked.

The theft...

I looked both ways, and seeing nobody watching, I stuck the box under my arm and walked on home. At home, I went to my secret hiding place, which was actually a crawl space underneath the back porch with a ceiling height of about two and a half feet. I knew that no adult would ever come to that small space. I opened the package and disappointingly found it to be made up of personalized Christmas cards. Having no use for them and with no concern for the people who paid for the cards and no integrity at the time, I left those Christmas cards underneath the porch at 455 Mt. Vernon Ave.

The cards are probably still there today.

But one of the little things that gnawed on me after I became a Christian was the fact that I had stolen the cards and never made proper restitution. A few years ago, I was driving near Erie, Pennsylvania, and thought it might not be too far out of the way to go to Rochester, New York, to make that long-overdue restitution. I was deeply disappointed when I found the residents of that house had moved away years before and left no forwarding address.

That episode taught me some things:

▲ You can't steal yourself happiness.

▲ Stuff that's stolen is usually not as enjoyable as stuff you've bought and paid for with your own money.

▲ If you're going to say you're sorry to somebody, say it while they're living.

26

How to Chase
the Customer Away

Car Dealers...

An example of abusive treatment of customers is the
time I went to look at a Mercedes-Benz. Having just recently become prosperous, I decided I needed a presti-
gious vehicle and went to my local Mercedes dealer in
Louisville, Kentucky. When I entered the showroom, I
walked around the car and looked at everything very
carefully. I looked and looked while the salesman sat
comfortably in the chair in his office. Finally, I walked to
his office which was about ten feet from the car. He saw
me every moment I was there. I asked him, "How much
does that car cost?"

He responded "You probably can't afford it."

I thought about that a moment and realized that if it
takes that kind of arrogant attitude to drive a Mercedes, I
guess I don't need one. I walked out.

Later I realized my mistake. I probably should have worn my pinstripe suit and made an appointment with the salesman. Or, maybe I should have had my secretary call his secretary and make an appointment for him to bring the car to me. Had I done that, I might have been able to purchase a Mercedes.

A Mercedes is in my price range. It's the attitude I can't afford.

More cars...

The **next car story** has to do with the fact that, in my lifetime, I've bought several new cars and several used ones. To date, I have never had a single salesman call me back to ask me if I was satisfied with my purchase or if I were ready for another one. They were more interested in the quick sale than the long term customer. In my lifetime I have owned 2 Volkswagens, 12 Buicks, 3 Dodges, 3 Lincolns, and 5 Cadillacs. I have never bought two cars from the same dealer. Think of how much money one dealer could have made had he checked on my customer satisfaction when I started.

Waitress...

After my supper at a restaurant, the bill was thirty-nine dollars and forty-eight cents. The waitress took my only fifty-dollar bill and brought the change: fifty-two cents and a ten-dollar bill. I looked at it and realized her change was correct, but I said, "Ma'am, I now have a problem. I had a nice dinner, and I am sitting on the option of giving you a fifty-two cent tip or a ten dollar tip, and I can't decide which one to give."

She looked at me a moment and said, "Sir, that's your problem, not mine. Let your conscience be your guide."

> # Had she been more concerned about my problem, I would have been more generous with the tip.

Had she been more concerned about my problem, I would have been more generous with the tip.

Back To The Restroom...

How about the bathroom doors that have closers that are so stiff that your child, if he gets in, may never get out?

Why are the paper towel bins always full? Are they too small or are they too infrequently emptied? Is the problem design or management?

In England, I visited a restroom that had a sign, CAUTION WATER VERY HOT. Being an engineer, I had a simple thought: There is some temperature-sensitive device somewhere in the plumbing circuit that controls the temperature. Sometime, somewhere, someone set the temperature too high. Why not locate that thermostat and reset it to one hundred ten degrees F. so that it would be comfortable for the customer, rather than scalding him? But that solution is too simple and too cheap and takes the customer's point of view. The solution provided by the building authorities was, in every bathroom throughout the building, to erect a CAUTION WATER VERY HOT sign.

In The Doctor's Office...

A few years ago I had an 11 a.m. appointment with the doctor. At 10:45, I called the doctor's office and asked if the doctor was on schedule. The nurse responded,

"Actually the doctor is behind. Could you come in at 1:30?"

I said, "Yes." At 1:15, I called and asked, "Will the doctor be ready to see me if I come in now?"

She responded, "I'm sure he will be caught up by 5 o'clock." At 4:45, I left home and arrived at the doctor's office, only to complete a forty-minute visit by 8:30 that evening. It would seem that a doctor could predict his schedule a little better after thirty-five years in the business. The doctor, however, stayed until 8:30 to finish the exam.

In another doctor's office...

My wife had an appointment at 8 a.m. Since she had a very painful cancer, she was very pleased to have the first appointment of the day, knowing she could get in and out quickly. At about 11 a.m., I got suspicious, and, seeing no new faces coming into the waiting room, I began to inquire of all those seated what time their appointment was and with which doctor. It turned out that nine different people had an 8 a.m. appointment with the doctor. I left a message with my phone number and said, "Call me at the hotel fifteen minutes before the doctor can see us."

In many Medical facilities...

There seems to be little regard for the cost to the patient of medical services. One of the most frustrating is the duplication of testing. The conversation goes like this: "But the last doctor already performed that same test." Response, "But we always like to do our own." If the gas station were like the doctor's office, each time I go in for a fill up, they would drain out all the old unused gasoline.

In Dr. Dancel's Office...

I arrived at 1 P.M. for an appointment. At 2:30, I asked the receptionist the following questions:

▲ Does the doctor intend to see me today?

▲ Will he see me soon?

▲ Is the doctor in the building?

▲ Where is the Doctor?

▲ What is the Doctor doing at home while I am waiting for him here?

▲ How soon do you expect him to finish cutting his grass?

▲ Could you call me at my office if and when he comes in?

Do you think I went back to him? Is it love of self or love of customer? Is it self-serving or other serving?

In seemingly every doctor's office the real operating principle seems to be "He will be late for his appointment; go sit down; stay out of our way; and be good. After all, our time is valuable, and yours is not worth anything."

> ## "After all, our time is valuable and yours is not worth anything."

The customer does not always get mad; he just gets chased to the competitor.

Post Office...

In a post office event, we received a notice that a package was too big to deliver. The notice said we would be required to drive to the post office to pick up the package. (You should know that this post office, following the infinite wisdom of most government agencies, is about twenty miles from our home. There are five post offices closer than the one that is required to handle our mail!)

My wife called the post office to request the delivery of the package and was told again that pick up would be necessary. Her comment to the post office representative was, "It seems to me that the post office should either have size limitations which cause it to refuse some packages for shipment, or, if it has accepted the package for shipment, it should be delivered." Later that day, the package actually was delivered to our home. My wife's comment? "Now do you see why I always ship UPS instead of USPS?"

License Branches...

Have you ever noticed that it's impossible to get prompt service in any government-operated franchise? Keeping the customer waiting must be the government standard procedure for keeping the taxpayer humble.

Hertz Rent A Car...

Why does Hertz only get about two percent of my car rental business? In about 1975 I was driving my personal car out of the Indianapolis airport when I was rear-ended by a Hertz employee. It seems that an attractive young lady had the youthful driver's attention drawn away from his driving. Hertz ended up paying for the repair to my rear ended car but would not reimburse my expense of substitute transportation without a receipt for rental. The reality was that there was no rental agency in my hometown and each day I drove my wife to and from work. When I explained that I did not have a receipt, they refused to pay any inconvenience cost. Had I understood the system, rather than trying to minimize the cost of the incident to Hertz, I probably should have rented a car for the three-week period from Avis, thus being able to produce a receipt. Since then ninety-five percent of my rentals have been from Avis.

Holiday Inn

Holiday Inn, until recently, had two problems: They were the largest retailer of pornographic movies through their in-room movie rental system. Their air-conditioning was only turned on in the hot summer and was not individually adjustable. For those two reasons, and mostly the first, Holiday Inn gets less than four percent of my hotel rentals.

The customer does not always get mad; he just gets chased to the competitor.

27

School Daze

Kindergarten

Like every kid going to kindergarten, there's the first day at school, being chased by the dog and not wanting to go. Yes, I was chased by a dog. I started school in LaPorte, Indiana, in January and then, when we moved to Rochester, New York, the question was, "Do we put him back to the beginning of a year that he's done half of or push him ahead?" So, I skipped half of second grade. That's why I still can't subtract.

Sixth Grade

Things went from bad to worse. In sixth grade, the teacher, Mr. Correll, was also the principal. He would occasionally get called out of class. I sat near the door. As soon as he left for the performance of one of his duties, the class trouble-causers started sticking their hands under their armpits and started making burping sounds with them. They did this for several minutes — in fact, almost every boy in the class was doing it. Since I didn't want to be left out, since I felt I really should do this because all the other guys were doing it, and they would probably like me more if I did, I started doing it too. I was having lots of fun, but I was apparently the only one who didn't notice the door open and the principal come through. That was the provocation of my being worked over with a paddle and the principal sending a note to my mother saying, "Your son will never amount to anything. He is the most trouble-causing child in his class."

Freshman

Things went from there to worse. Every year I would try out for basketball and football, and I would always make third string on the football team because there were not enough kids to fill all the positions. I'd always get cut from the basketball team because they always had plenty of good people to go out for it. I never did play in football until my freshman year because I happened to, that year, become the second string center.

The history behind that is simply this: the first string center was so good, so strong, so tough, he never got tired; therefore, he always played all of every game. But, luck would have it, he broke his leg a day or so before a game, and that was my chance because I was the only person who knew all of the plays so they had to play me. And I did play one game. Then the guy, I guess because I did so poorly, healed up from his broken leg and played the next week. He probably played better than I did — he could play better with a cast on his leg than I could without.

My career as a football star continued through the end of the season until some of my friends on the football team decided to let me in on the inner circle, and they decided to take me on a snipe hunt. Well, they didn't think I knew what a snipe hunt was, and I didn't know who was going to be hunting the snipes, but I discovered that I was going to be left holding the bag. They let me out of the car and drove off.

> **But I discovered that I was going to be left holding the bag.**

After I had been sleeping with a gunny sack under my head for four or five hours, they came back beating on pans and chasing the imaginary snipes to me. I thought that was really kind of them, but I had also decided to get even with Bob. I threw myself into a nearby ditch, covering myself totally with mud and wallered in it. Then I chased the imaginary snipes. I got into his car, and totally covered the back seat with mud. So, when they took me home, they were all laughing at me because I didn't catch any of the snipes and was left holding the bag, but I got my revenge. I am now sorry, Bob, please forgive me.

Math...

Then the freshman class had a math contest. All the smart kids were going to study for the school-wide test but I, being a C student, knew there was no chance of my scoring high on the test. My friends, one of which was very likely going to win the contest, asked if I was going to take the test — kind of making fun of me knowing full well that I didn't stand a ghost of a chance.

He said, "Hey Floyd, if you take the test, you could get out of Miss Anderson's Latin class." Then I thought about how embarrassing Latin class would be without the half dozen really smart kids for me to hide behind. They had been studying for weeks for this test. They studied during every available moment before and after class, and during study hall. They wanted to win the math contest. To escape Latin, I decided to take the test too.

Everybody was shocked when I came up with the highest score. The teacher started giving me A's instead of the C's that I deserved. Apparently, the other kids remembered what they studied. I simply reasoned on unfamiliar material. Never again, except in mathematics, did I do anything academically superior, but I did get no less than third place in all the math contests in high school from that year forward.

Junior

I must tell you about Mr. Bell. He is the man who taught me Chemistry and Physics. I enjoyed trying to make the teachers uncomfortable by asking trap questions; that helped me to feel smarter. It was Mr. Bell whom I tried to embarrass that day to boost my ego. He explained Ohm's law relating to resistors, batteries, and D.C. circuits. I asked him about a superconductor connected to a battery, suggesting that it would yield an infinite current flow which was logically impossible.

> **I highly respected Mr. Bell all the rest of the days of his life.**

That would have repudiated what he had said earlier in class. He then took about twenty-five minutes out to explain to me in great detail and in the presence of everybody else the solution to the problem that I had posed. He is the man to whom I would give credit for igniting my interest in Physics. I highly respected Mr. Bell all the rest of the days of his life. You see, while going through life, you never know who is looking up to you. When you have a chance to teach somebody something, give them additional knowledge to work with. By all means, take advantage of that God-given opportunity.

Senior

Yes, it was my senior English teacher Miss McHenry who made us memorize a poem or scripture every day. She

> **She did not know that our personalities might be warped (according to current educational standards) by our exposure to moral values.**

did not know that our personalities might be warped (according to current educational standards) by our exposure to moral values. Just for the record, she required the memorization of the Ten Commandments.

I was sixteen when I met Katie Anthony, the girl in the choir who was so odd. When I asked her twice why she was so odd, she finally said, "I'm a Christian." It was after two and a half hours of her telling me about God's Son that I became a Christian.

All those personal experiences in school have caused me to ponder a continuous question. Every time I meet a successful type—a president, a CEO, a rich guy, an artist, a scholar— I wonder if this person like me, is also a walking contradiction. Did he have a teacher who prophesied, "You'll never amount to anything"? I have remembered the words. Despite all those predictions, some of us do make it. Based on this, I rather suspect that some of the students in schools now might actually grow up to be real people with some degree of success.

Let's ponder this even deeper. What is the possibility that our lives are in the hands of someone wiser than all of us put together?

28

Lessons from the Bunny Slope

Fear is a terrible thing, and I have spent too much of my life being fearful. I was afraid of failing. I was afraid of falling. I was afraid of crashing. I don't have much fear anymore.

Did you ever go skiing? Do you know what the bunny slope is? That's the small hill for small kids. Do you think I would be embarrassed if I went on the bunny slope? I was, so I went over to the big kid's hill. After riding the ski lift to the top, I became terrified. I removed my skis, walked toward the edge of the hill, then got down on my hands and knees and crawled to the precipice and looked straight down fifty feet before the ledge even faintly resembled a hill. Discovering that riding the ski lift back down the hill was un-authorized, my only option was to reinstall my skis and do it.

Some one hundred twenty-five falls later that evening I rode home in excruciating pain. But I didn't experience the embarrassment of the bunny slope.

Pride cometh before a fall.

29

Embarrass Your Way
to Confidence

Have you ever been embarrassed? You have a runner in your hose; does it bother you? I don't care. It does not affect my relationship to you and it does not affect the beauty of your smile. So I don't care if you have a runner; it makes no difference.

One of the reasons we are not as successful as we could and should be is that success requires boldness. One of the reasons we are not as bold as we could and should be, for greatest effectiveness, is that we are afraid of becoming embarrassed when our boldness causes us to stand out. We fear that we will fail; that's why we do not try.

I wouldn't mind coming to a meeting with a big, black smudge on my shirt, except when I have to stand in front of everybody, I assume the only thing they see is the smudge on my shirt. So, I cover up the smudge by holding my hand in a weird position. I think then that everyone is staring at my hand, and then I wonder what's on the back of my hand. It is fear of being embarrassed that causes us not to be as bold as we could be. It detracts from our greatest effectiveness. It is lack of boldness that detracts from our success.

What are some of the obstacles to boldness? What are the inhibitions to venturing out and trying something new? What are the experiences you have in life that cause you to withdraw from opportunities? What are the things that cause fear and introversion?

Common fears ...

1. Fear of appearing to be impolite.
2. Fear of offending.
3. Fear of embarrassing others.
4. Fear of looking poor or of low class.
5. Fear of appearing to be arrogant.
6. Fear of getting lost.
7. Fear of confusion.
8. Fear of getting stuck in the snow.
9. Fear of giving the wrong answer.
10. Fear of breaking something.
11. Fear of failure.
12. Fear of looking worse than I am.
13. Fear of admitting your insecurity.
14. Fear of getting a speeding ticket.
15. Fear of leaving the keys locked in the car.
16. Fear of overdrawing the bank account.
17. Fear of being late to church.
18. Fear of going to the meeting on the wrong day.
19. Fear of misunderstanding a simple instruction.
20. Fear of tearing the seat out of your pants.

21. Fear of having stomach cramps, diarrhea, or vomiting.
22. Fear of picking up the wrong map.
23. Fear of taking a wrong turn and getting lost.
24. Fear of getting stuck in sand on the beach.
25. Fear of asking for a date and being refused.
26. Fear of having to sleep in the car because you forgot to make the hotel reservation.
27. Fear of having to sleep in the car because you could not afford a hotel.
28. Fear of having nothing to say.
29. Fear of saying nothing.
30. Fear of getting stuck in the sand on the beach again, after you got towed out last night.
31. Fear of forgetting which car you drove to the airport.
32. Fear of not being able to find your car at the airport after the snow.
33. Fear of losing your place in the music and having to stop singing.
34. Fear of driving five hundred miles up the wrong side of the Nile River.
35. Fear of knocking off your bride's veil during the wedding.
36. Fear of your test score being one of the lowest in the class.
37. Fear of others laughing at your clothes.
38. Fear of not knowing the answer when the teacher calls on you.
39. Fear of falling into a septic tank.
40. Fear of dragging a line of toilet paper when you leave the rest room.
41. Fear of your pants being unzipped while singing at church.

42. Fear of trying to spit at the dentist's office and missing the bowl.

43. Fear of passing a loud amount of gas as you sneeze.

44. Fear of inviting folks over for steaks and finding there's no gas in the grill.

45. Fear of the electricity being shut off when you have a house full of company.

46. Fear of the car you loaned to a friend breaking down.

47. Fear of forgetting you invited company and you're already gone for the weekend.

48. Fear of forgetting your anniversary.

49. Fear of spilling the tray full of soft drinks you're carrying across the restaurant.

50. Fear of being left holding the bag on a snipe hunt.

51. Fear of being the last one chosen.

52. Fear of losing your plane tickets.

53. Fear of not making the honor roll.

54. Fear of taking more than four years to finish college.

55. Fear of getting cut from the team.

56. Fear of not qualifying for the scholarship.

57. Fear of not being able to see.

58. Fear of not being able to hear conversations.

59. Fear of your car having rust on it.

60. Fear of someone discovering that your pastor doesn't have a Ph.D.

61. Fear of losing the election.

62. Fear of having to put stuff back at the grocery because you don't have enough money.

63. Fear of your printer not being able to do all the fancy stuff that your friend's printer does.

64. Fear of your voice cracking on the high note.

65. Fear of burning the steaks (after you found more gas for the grill!)

66. Fear of giving last year's unwanted gift back to the person who gave it to you.

So you don't try...

You become so fearful that you are afraid to try anything, lest there be any misunderstanding. I made all of the above mistakes and more, but I learned from them. I did not quit; I gained confidence. I lost self-consciousness.

Fear of not seeing the end from the beginning holds many people

Just remember, "Good judgment comes from experience. And experience comes from experiences due to bad judgment. And bad judgment comes from lack of experience. And lack of experience comes from not trying. And not trying comes from fear of embarrassment." Therefore success only comes to those whose fear of embarrassment has been overcome.

You're driving your car along the flat beaches in Florida. You know that where the water has been recently, it's safe to drive. Where the sand is loose and dry, that's where you get stuck. It is fear of getting stuck driving across the loose sand that keeps most people from the great pleasure of driving on the beach.

Fear of getting stuck is what causes people to stay home when it snows.

Fear of making something worse than what is hampers bold involvement.

Fear of not seeing the end from the beginning holds many people back. Before they do anything at all, some people need to be able to see each step along the path. They need to know that their path can be successfully executed without their getting hit by any stray bullets, without stepping in a mud puddle, and without anything in the project going wrong. They tend to focus so much on safety and security that they lose the opportunity. They give up opportunity for security.

Obstacles to boldness include having fear that it may be against the rules. Fear that there may be a law against it. "You can't do that because you have to have a license." Some people go through life saying, "The only things that I can do are those things that are specifically allowed." That's totalitarianism. That's the Soviet police state.

My approach to life is, "We can do everything except that which is specifically denied." (Of course within the guidelines that God has set.) The issue is, "Are we slaves or are we free?" That is Americanism.

Strength to Stand Alone...

You're at a party, and the rest of the guys are doing drugs or drinking. Everybody says that you should do it, too, but you say, "No." Something makes you think that if you say no, you will embarrass yourself by making yourself completely different from everybody else. You will probably arrive home safely after the party. It is in being willing to embarrass yourself that you achieve a greater level of safety.

Remember my story about when I was flying my airplane, tired, and was caught in a night thunderstorm, low on fuel, having been up seventeen hours. I was flying along over central Kentucky. The thunderstorm developed unexpectedly. I was not instrument rated; I didn't know how to fly through clouds. I didn't know how to fly when I couldn't see, and I didn't have enough instruments in the airplane to handle that sort of flying anyway.

But I was willing to be embarrassed by violating some rules, by landing on a highway, by facing the ridicule of everybody who knew of it. And, in the process of being willing to be embarrassed, I saved my life. You can not imagine how much harassment I got. "Hey Coates, don't you know where the airport is?" But I *walked* away from a bad situation because I was willing to be embarrassed.

If you're going to be successful, you've got to be bold. The prime hindrance to boldness is embarrassment. I boldly decided, "I'm going to land this airplane on the interstate highway." If you are going to be effective for God or good or your customer, you must be willing to embarrass yourself and be candid and honest.

> **I was so embarrassed while I was going through school because I knew the answer so little of the time.**

When I was in school, I was a C or D student. I was the guy to whom the teacher would say, "How many can tell me what six times three is?" And I would sit there with my hands folded very reverently, like I was praying. Actually, I was trying to be very inconspicuous. I was staring at a blank spot on the wall hoping the teacher wouldn't see me. Then she said, "How many know what two plus three is?" Because I knew the answer my hand shot up in the air. I wanted to be recognized when I knew the answer.

Study to Avoid Embarrassment...

I was so embarrassed while I was going through school because I knew the answer so little of the time. The only reason I studied was that I just wanted to prevent embarrassment. I didn't memorize my Latin words because I wanted to know their meaning. The only reason I studied Latin, Algebra, Geometry, Trigonometry, Chemistry, English, remedial knitting, or anything else was to prevent embarrassment. I knew the teacher would call on me sometime, and I'd again have to say, "I don't know," in front of everyone.

Embarrassment is one of the beautiful things that helps us through life if we use it right. I feared being called upon so I studied more. The transformation in my life came when, as a thirteen-year-old freshman in high school, I started studying homework four hours a day.

To learn the value of saving, you have to save. To learn the value of tithing, you have to tithe. To enjoy the value of skiing, you have to ski. To expand your skills, you have to stretch and be willing to be embarrassed by the limitations of your skill. You do not become rich by burying your cash in the ground; you make it work for you by investing and taking risks.

Embarrassment sometimes provides some unexpected, beautiful results. I realized I had very poor recall of facts, while I had quite sharp ability to reason logically. I don't remember what I thought yesterday. I don't remember what I did a moment ago, but I can rethink logically something probably quicker than most folks I know.

I learned on a school-wide math exam that when dealing with unfamiliar material, I could react better and more quickly than most folks. The other guys who studied for the math exam re-studied information they had already learned. I was halfway able to work problems, the concepts of which had never been explained before, mostly because I was willing to guess and take the risk. And, by being willing to be embarrassed, knowing full well that I would get the lowest grade in the school-wide math test, I got the unexpected pleasure of getting the highest grade. Being willing to embarrass yourself occasionally achieves unexpected results.

Being willing to be embarrassed sometimes builds rapport with others. I had to talk to my wife today to find out how to spell rapport. She taught me the difference between rapport and report. She was happy to have the opportunity for a moment of conversation where she out-smarted me. I lost nothing in the exchange. When you have the almost- spelling-bee-champion of Alabama as your wife, you become accustomed to being humbled.

> **Being accustomed to being embarrassed, it makes it easier to "just say 'no' " when everybody else seems to be doing wrong.**

I sometimes purposely appear to be a country bumpkin. It often helps make other folks feel more comfortable. I have learned to be very comfortable with embarrassment. I think I do the crowd a great service by asking the stupid questions that others wanted to ask. Being willing to step out of my comfort zone has made possible several things. I have been the Republican nominee for U. S. Congress in southern Indiana. I am owner of two corporations employing one hundred thirty-seven people, and have been self-employed for many years. I have traveled much of the world. I am a multi-engine instrument rated pilot, the world's best plastic molder, and a lot more things I am too humble to admit. But somebody said, "Man, if a guy as stupid as Coates can do that, surely I can, too." That is the goal: to help others up the ladder of success.

Just because you are bungling and clumsy and ugly and poor and stupid and you don't have any money and you have holes in your socks and you have dirt on your shirt, don't use any of those as excuses for failure.

Get in the habit... Just say "No"...

Being accustomed to being embarrassed and being comfortable with being laughed at makes it easier to stand alone for a right cause. It makes it easier to "just say 'no' " when everybody else seems to be doing wrong.

30

What I Learned about Learning

One Saturday morning I was lying in my bedroom wondering what the inscription on my tombstone would read.

Epitaph...

"He lived. He died. He didn't make any difference."
I was depressed with the thought.
I wondered what my problems were, and I listed them. I was poor, ugly, stupid and had no friends. I thought I would never amount to anything, but the thought occurred to me that no one could possibly have more than a thirteen-year head start on me.
How many of you think you are beautiful? The rest of us feel we are ugly. The rest of us feel that God shorted us somehow. I said, "God, you messed up when you made me, but I can change that." I thought, "What must I do to solve my ugliness?" I realized then that there really wasn't much I could do with my God-given appearance, but

I could go from taking a bath once a week to once a day. And I could go from changing my underwear once a week to once a day. (You want me to be truthful, don't you? This did not change my handsomeness any, but it did make me slightly more pleasant to be around.)

I found that if I were to have friends, I had to be genuinely interested in what they were doing. But it seems as if I have generally continued to be more interested in what I was doing than what they were doing, so I still don't have very many friends. If you want to read a good book on the subject, it's entitled *How to Win Friends and Influence People* by Dale Carnegie. If you go around beating up people and tearing up their stuff and humiliating, embarrassing, frustrating, irritating and demeaning them, then they won't be your friends. If you are concerned, kind, courteous and helpful to people, they will be your friends. You share your toys with me, and I will share my toys with you.

I think God said it something like, "It is more blessed to give than to receive."

Coates paraphrased as follows, "If you concentrate on giving, the getting will take care of itself."

Zig Ziglar says, "You'll get all the things you want if you help enough people get all they want."

I was stupid. More accurately, I was ignorant. Then I realized that if I would read I could get smart, too. Knowing that all knowledge is contained within the encyclopedia, I began to read all the way from A

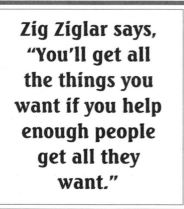

Zig Ziglar says, "You'll get all the things you want if you help enough people get all they want."

to Electricity. It was then that I discovered that the encyclopedia didn't have all the information about everything. I went to the library and started reading about electricity, which led me to motors, which led me to telegraph and radio and television. It was after that that I started my first business, Coates' Radio Repair.

Back when I was in the fifth grade, I always sat in class waiting for the teacher to ask questions. If I knew the answer, I would wave my hand violently in the air trying to get her attention. But if I didn't know the answer, I would sit frozen, staring at the wall, hoping not to establish eye contact with the teacher, hoping the teacher wouldn't see me sitting in my chair.

But I found that when I read more, when I studied more, when I did my homework, I could raise my hand more frequently. I received C's and D's and a few F's all the way through grade school and junior high.

Turning Point...

When I became a freshman, my C's and D's in Math and English went to A's. What happened? I started reading, that's all. I did about four hours of homework each night.

Even though I smell better, I'm still ugly. I don't know whether I have friends or not – you have to ask them about that; and I may still be stupid, but at least I am a well-read stupid person.

If you thirst for knowledge, it will come.

Reading is not the only knowledge input. My wife reads thirteen hundred words per minute. I read one hundred twenty-five words per minute. There are audio tapes, video tapes, sermons, seminars, speeches, radio broadcasts, educational TV programs, salesmen, friends, magazines, newspapers, the web, labels and manuals. The inputs are sometimes hours at a time, sometimes only seconds – but constant – every day. Each moment of learning adds up.

All additional knowledge makes you more valuable to yourself and your customers.

31

Power Lost – "Power Outages at the Coates' House"

The Coates, in our usual style, had invited a house full of company to visit. This night was no different. The guests were evangelist Ray McCrary, his family and a handful of others. I got home around 8:30 p.m. and the guests were to arrive later. I noticed that the lights were out in the house and reached for a switch, but no lights came on. As is quite common in the hot summer at Coates' house, there was a power outage. Not to be terribly inconvenienced, I lit some oil lamps and began to prepare for the guests and called the electric utility, Public Service Indiana.

Since I couldn't see to read the phone book, I dialed from memory. Calling in my usual style, I said, "Hi, this is Floyd Coates. I'm sorry I didn't pay my light bill last month and I beg for mercy. If I promise to pay my bill tomorrow, will you turn my lights on tonight?" The guy said, "Hello?" I repeated my statement. He said, "OK. I'll turn your lights back on. Why didn't you pay your light bill?" I said, "Oh you know how it goes, you run out of cash and all that stuff. The neighbors have lights on, but I do not, so it must be simply because I didn't pay my bill." We hung up.

As I thought about that, I realized that the guy, representing a major electric utility, did not have a very professional demeanor, and I wonder if he may have taken my joking style as an idle prank call. So I called again. "Hi, this is Floyd Coates. I called a little while ago and reported my electricity out, and I was wondering when you guys are going to turn it back on." There was some ambiguous answer on the other end of the line. The guy really sounded stupid. Something was uncannily weird about the conversations. Maybe the guy was newly hired by the utility. He was very unprofessional in his demeanor, and he was somewhat accommodating but not really. Something was wrong!

Pay the bill...

So I decided to call the corporate headquarters. I called Mom (she had lights) and asked her to look up the electric utility's corporate headquarters phone number. I called the corporate headquarters, and they transferred me to a guy who said that they had not received any reports of my power being out. But he said, "May I check?" The guy came back on the line later and said, "Yes sir. Your power was shut off several days ago because you haven't paid your bill." In fact, we had been out of town for several days.

> **"If I promise to pay my bill tomorrow, will you turn my lights on tonight?"**

I said, "Hey, we have a problem. I have lived here for thirty years; I've bought electricity from you for forty years, and at this house and at my company together, I spend approximately $250,000 per year for electricity from your company. I own real estate; I'm not likely to move. It is reasonable to me, since I have a house full of company coming in a few minutes, for you to turn my electricity on tonight, and I'll pay you tomorrow."

The lady said, "I'm sorry, sir. Our business hours are 8:00 a.m. - 4:30 p.m. You may pay your bill then."

I said, "Grumble, grumble, grumble."

Joke...

By now, our guests had arrived. "Hey, Coates, what's going on?"

I said, "I didn't pay my light bill."

"You what? Ha Ha!" he laughed. Three hours later, everybody was standing around the house with candles and oil lamps and sweat, because it was in the middle of the summer. The entire evening was spent without the convenience of air conditioning, ice crusher, radio, hot water, air conditioning, TV, VCR, lights, fans, air conditioning, exhaust fan, garage door opener, clock, computer, freezer, refrigerator, air conditioning, and a million other things that require electricity. I had a house full of guests who insisted that it was a prank. Never, never, even to this day would Ray McCrary believe me that I didn't pay my bill!

I called and awoke my secretary, Missy, at home and explained to her the problem. She agreed that she hadn't paid the electric bill but assured me that she would be at the electric company's office first thing the next morning with cash — small, unmarked bills.

To be sure that it was truly a disconnect for non-payment of bill rather than power failure, I used a flashlight to point up to the utility pole's entrance to the house. It showed a disconnected fuse link, which only the electric company could turn back on.

> # All twelve of us huddled around a six-inch TV in our living room.

Survival...

Near midnight, I ran wires from the battery of the car to the living room of the house. I dug up from a stash of electrical devices a twelve-volt TV and VCR and watched "The Gods are Angry." All twelve of us huddled around a six-inch TV in our living room. After the movie, I disconnected the TV and VCR and ran long wires into the master bedroom where the master (me) had the benefit of a twelve-volt fan running until the car battery went dead.

Communicate...

Regardless of how good a customer you may be and how good your past record may be, you need to communicate with your power source on a regular basis.

That's the whole lesson of Christianity. The Power Source is available to all of us and is even better than the utility company. He even makes house calls in the middle of the night. But we still need to stay in touch. That's called prayer. Staying in touch with the Power Source, is a sure-fire method for brightening up our lives.

And, this power source is free.

As a supplier it is the occasional late delivery, bad product, or billing error that destroys a relationship.

32

Why Communists Don't Understand Customer Service!

In March of 2000 I gave a series of lectures on the subject of Customer Service at a University in Prague. They had no concept of customer service. They did not know what a customer was and they did not know how to serve.

They had no concept of the customer because their government did not recognize the concept of private property ownership. The concept of private property was created by God. He said, "Thou shalt not steal." The recognition of property rights is implied by the definition of stealing.

If you wish the property of another, you have only three ways to get it: steal it, pass a law, or earn it.

The first is to steal it. All societies have determined that for one man to take another's property without his consent is wrong.

The second is to have a law passed that would take from him and give to you. The danger of a Democracy was clearly pointed out by our founding fathers. In a Democracy a majority of the people can get a benefit from the taxpayers by the collective force of government. A law is passed benefiting a group. A tax is passed to cause some other class of people to pay for it. The coercive force of government collects the tax from the taxpayer. That government then determines who should get the benefits. Which brings us to a salient point. What is the proper role of government?

The right of a man to defend his household from a thief by force is universally accepted. The establishment of a police force to protect a community from thieves is also universally accepted. However, when the collective force of police and legislature is used to transfer property from those who have earned it to give to those who did not earn it, that is a perversion of the law and an unjust act of government. It is a good law that provides for the defense of individuals and their property. It is a bad law which takes by force from one group of people and gives to another, regardless of how well meaning the legislator or the law.

The third way to gain wealth is to earn it. That is to provide a service or product to another so that he would be willing to make a voluntary exchange. How can this be in a society that does not recognize the right of an individual to own property? In a society where commerce is not a free exchange from one individual to another, there is no incentive for

If you wish the property of another, you have only three ways to get it:

...steal it,

...pass a law,

...or earn it.

the individual to perform better. The concept of earning for disposable income is unheard of in a socialist or communist society. To get the other person's money you must provide something he wants. If you satisfy his need, he will satisfy yours.

The Communists have not learned the principle of service as defined by God. Good customer service comes from the heart. It is God who can change the heart of man. The standard of God's relationship of man to man is that of serving. Serve one another as if you are serving God directly through the deed and person in front of you. This is God's definition of service.

33

I COULD
HAVE KILLED MYSELF

I was just learning about electricity and was the proud owner of a train set. This, of course, was the old-style train set that had three tracks with one of the conductors in the middle of the track, not like the fancy models made these days. But with the train came a transformer that converted 110 volt AC current into about five to twelve volts. This, of course, had the advantage of reducing the voltage to a safe level suitable for toy trains.

A Thousand Volts...

Being ignorant of electrical theory, but learning, I thought, "I wonder if this thing could operate backwards. If I connect the wires that usually go to the track and plug them into the wall receptacle and take the end of the transformer that had the plug on it and connect it to the track, I wonder if the train would work or would it run backwards or what would it do?" About then I made

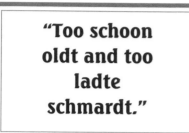

"Too schoon oldt and too ladte schmardt."

the final connection to the wall socket. With a zap of spark and a puff of smoke and the terrible smell of burned varnish insulation of the transformer, the transformer died. I later learned in the Physics class that what came out the plug for the moment it lasted was between one thousand and two thousand volts. I'm glad I was not connected to it.

I am only then reminded that my father used to tell me a German quotation: "Too schoon oldt and too ladte schmardt."

34

Proverbs According to Coates

Folks like me who have short attention spans have difficulty with great philosophical truths and intellectual depths.

I heard it said of a speaker, "Never have I gone down so deep, stayed under so long and come up so dry."

Even in my own speaking, it was said, "Floyd, your speech was both interesting and original. But the interesting parts were not original, and the original parts were not interesting." Below, I want to list several short pithy guiding principles, concepts, and ideas that have helped to formulate my lifestyle or to explain it. I can remember the source of only few of them. They are mostly self-explanatory.

Principles of Urgency...

When given a great opportunity, a young man responded, "But sir, there's not enough time." The old man responded, "The average person always requires more time. That's why they're average."

"Going through life is like walking across a river on floating logs. The more lively you step, the less likely you are to get wet."

"There's a time in every project to shoot the engineer and get on with production."

"Ready, shoot, aim." Some feel this is reckless, but actually, some people can get off three shots while others are aiming their first.

"Rome wasn't built in a day because I wasn't there." I am frequently criticized by my staff for feeling that today's non-urgent project needs to be dealt with immediately. Often non-urgent but important projects never get done.

"Have a propensity toward action."

"Strike while the iron is hot."

Handy Advice...

"Have at least a half a tank of gas in your car in the winter." It is very handy when you spend a night in a snowdrift.

"It is the eighth grade level mistakes that I make that kill me." Though I have my degree in Physics, the technical problems, the personal problems, virtually every expensive, painful mistake I have made was an eighth grade level problem.

"That's why some make ten and some make fifty dollars per hour." That relates to different pay rates folks receive because of their abilities and efforts. Some deserve a lot more because they achieve a lot more. This is certainly counter to our welfare state mentality.

"It's good to have church candy. Did you know that lifesavers are good during the sermons? The wrappers don't make any noise either."

"What tastes better than six Pepsis per day? One per week."

"Had it been easy, I would have done it myself."

"The first bowl of soup always tastes better than the second."

> **"The first bowl of soup always tastes better than the second."**

Principles To Live By...

"The only causes worth fighting for are the lost causes. If victory is inevitable, the battle does not need your help."

"Put it together – clean, oiled, and tight." My father never knew much about mechanical principles. He did not know why things worked. He seemed to have a life-long occupation doing mechanical things he did not understand. But if you do the basic things very well, most of your problems will go away, be they mechanical, personal, or financial.

Absolutes...

"There must be absolutes:

▲ Lines you will not cross.

▲ Prices you will not pay.

▲ Things you will not do.

▲ Places you will not go.

▲ Things you will not say."

If you establish a set of absolutes in your life or business, you always have some basis for decision making. Just because the absolutes above are expressed negatively, they must not be construed as negative principles. They each identify very positive concepts.

"Which is it? All that is not expressly forbidden is allowed, or all that is not expressly allowed is forbidden." The difference between those two is an expression of freedom.

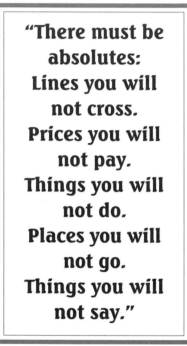

"There must be absolutes: Lines you will not cross. Prices you will not pay. Things you will not do. Places you will not go. Things you will not say."

"During time of crisis, confusion and anarchy, the first person to the microphone will be the leader." Those of us who are too timid and too slow to express our views but whose views are much more intelligent become the followers of him who first goes to the microphone.

"What's your crisis? If you don't have one, find one."

"It's not the size of the dog in the fight but the size of the fight in the dog that is important."

"How can we improve the (person, company, country, world) today?"

"Lead like you would like to be led."

"What's your current crisis?...if you're not working on a crisis, then go find one. These days I guess they call it 'Continuous improvement.'"

"Memorize your charge card number. That way you can place a phone order for something you just saw on TV without having to get out of bed.

"All that glistens ain't gold."

"So you want my money? Here's how to get it! (Treat me just like you'd treat yourself)"

"Explain to a customer what is wrong with his design three times. After that do your best to make his plan work."

"The golden rule: whoever follows it, gets the gold."

"The best salesmen are the ones that don't try to sell, but who solve problems."

"All the world really needs is...Good Customer Service."

35

Spiders
and What They Had for Lunch

Evolutionary Theory Lacks Creativity...

What about spiders?

Once upon a time a spider was sitting on a downspout wishing that he had legs so he could walk around like all the other animals. Having great faith in evolution, over a period of roughly 50 million years, he patiently evolved himself a set of legs. It was neat, because then he could walk around like all of the other animals. That was just terrific! But, his life was lacking. What he really wanted to do was spin a web. Over a period of about 40 million years, he evolved a spinner so that he could spin a web. The problem was, after he spun the web, a mosquito flew by and flew into the web and bounced off.

The spider said, "That's not going to work very well." He thought about that for a while and said, "Wouldn't it be really neat if I could evolve myself a glue gland so that I could smear glue on my web?" By the way, did you know that in a spider web, the parts of the web that go around have glue on them and the ones that go out radially from the center don't have glue on them?

So he evolved himself a glue gland over about 30 million years. He finally evolved a wonderful system designed such that the next time a mosquito flew by and got caught in the web, he could have his first lunch. Could you imagine living without eating for 120 million years? I could not. Had the

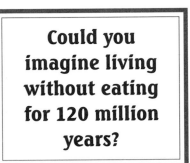

Could you imagine living without eating for 120 million years?

mosquito not come by that day, how much longer could the spider have gone without eating? How could the spider have had kids without having any food for them to eat? Why should a spider evolve a spinner if it could find food some other way?

Eve Husbandless 63,000,000 Years...

Some feel that Eve evolved first. She lived for nearly sixty-three million years until Adam evolved from an ape. Fortunately, he had the wherewithal to help her have children. They had several children including Cain, Abel, and daughters. Can you imagine where we would be if Eve had died of loneliness one hundred years before Adam evolved? The human race would never have occurred.

It takes a strong religious faith in evolution to believe that the first woman could live that long while Adam was evolving. How did Adam find Eve? What if he had evolved on the other side of the world? What if he had been afraid of Eve? What if he did not know how to

> **It takes a strong religious faith in evolution to believe that the first woman could live that long while Adam was evolving.**

produce kids? What if the kids did not know where to get lunch when they were born? What if Adam did not know to cut the cord?

Evolution is Bad Science...

Evolution leaves too many unanswered questions such as these to be credible to this physicist.

Evolution is bad science; no one has ever seen it happen. No one has ever caused evolution to occur. It is not repeatable nor predictable; therefore, it is not science; it is religion.

Creation by Design...

I am a Creationist. In a book entitled, *The Book of Beginnings,* God is quoted as having said, "Let the earth bring forth the living creature after his kind." That means spiders recreate spiders, apes recreate apes, people recreate people, snakes recreate snakes, and horses recreate horses. There are variations within kinds of animals such as in color, size, temperament, and shape. Dogs have an almost infinite variety of characteristics. But after all the variation, they are still dogs. There are wide variations in cats, but they are all cats. Cats do not become turtles.

"And God made the beasts of the earth after his kind and the cattle after their kind." God must have anticipated discussion about evolution. He explained that if you are a horse, your father, your grandfather, and your great-grandfather were also horses. God was talking to Jesus when He said, "Let us make man in our image." God did not claim to be a horse or a frog. The Father, the Son and people have a common image.

Who is Boss??? God or man?...

The argument about creation/evolution is important. If man can make himself believe that there was no creator, then there is no supreme authority. Man is logically able to determine right and wrong for himself. It is called moral relativism or secularism. If there is no God, there can be no evil in society, just difference from the norm. There can be no absolutes of good and evil, right and wrong, if there is no God. If there is no God, then right and wrong is whatever man says it is.

If man can make himself believe that there was no creator, then there is no supreme authority. Man is logically able to determine right and wrong

And we will return to the Dark Ages.

If a man accepts that he is a creation of God, it is his obligation to find out what God's plan for him is. Who is superior, the created or the Creator? It is man's obligation to find what God wants Him to do in his life.

Later testimony of our origin is found in the Constitution of the United States and the Declaration of Independence which says, "We hold these truths to be self-evident." Self-evident means they're so absolutely simple and obvious, there's no real reason to discuss them.

"That all men are created." Created? No question in the minds of our founding fathers about how we got here. "That they were endowed by their Creator." Those folks believed we were created by a Creator.

We, in America, are unique. We have created our government to be our servant, not our master. The problem is most people think we're supposed to be slaves of government or of a ruling class. Well, that may be in Communist countries; that may be in various dictatorships; but it does not happen to be the form of government that we have here in the United States. We are endowed by our Creator with certain inalienable rights and, as Christians, we believe we were created by the hand of God.

Science is the study of observable, repeatable events. Evolution is neither observable nor repeatable.

I wasn't there when we were created. I cannot say, scientifically, that we were created. I have not seen evolution occur, and nobody else has either. You can't scientifically say there was evolution. If you believe in evolution, you must accept it by faith. You were not there to observe it. Science is the study of observable, repeatable events. Evolution is neither observable nor repeatable. It is a fantasy. Our world shows striking evidence of a master design. Thus there must be a designer.

Our schools teach us to have faith in evolution. I have a problem. I don't have that much faith. Now, if I were just an ordinary old spider and I were running around, I could not see myself going 120 million years without lunch.

Our world shows striking evidence of a master design. Thus there must be a designer.

36

GOD Is!
Therefore He Should Be Boss

Unanswered questions...

Several questions must be asked:
Is death really final?
If there is an afterlife, what is its nature?
If there are heaven and hell, what are their natures?
If heaven is desirable, then what are the qualifications to enter?
How did we get here?
Did we evolve from a huge mass of energy and an explosion in which inert helium gas evolved into oxygen and uranium?
What is the authority on such matters?
If we were not created, what is the basis for authority in our race, who is right and who is wrong? What is the basis for morality in that case?
If we were created, should the designer and builder have authority over his creation?

If not he, whom?
What is the plan of God?
What is the source of our information?
Is the Bible true?

Is there a better historical document than the collection of books called the Bible?

If qualification for heaven involves Christ, did He really exist?

If we were created and if God created us (the only person who claimed to have created the world is God), and if He is our authority, and if there are heaven and hell, then it behooves us to try to understand His plan.

We were created or we evolved...

If we were created, then there is a Creator, and if that Creator had a plan for His creation, what is that plan? Is that plan in the Bible? What does it say about our responsibilities toward others?

Only after we have dealt with some of the major questions is it appropriate to deal with the small questions. You do not erect the walls before you build the foundation. After the foundation is established, most of the small questions answer themselves.

More unanswered questions...

It is interesting that the secular view of history totally denies the existence of Israel, the historical battle between Ishmael and Jacob. All over Israel there are land marks depicting "the place where...," "the birth place of...," "the death place of...," "there are legends about...," multiple eye witness accounts of many events, etc., yet secular history seems to ignore all events that point to anything mentioned in scripture.

A few days before his death, King Hussein of Jordan said that he was descended from Ishmael and that his countrymen should try to get along peacefully with the descendants of Jacob; Israelites and the Jordanians should live in peace. He attested to the common knowledge of historical events dating back to about 3,000 BC. It is logical if there were an Ishmael, then there was a Joseph, and if a Joseph, then a Noah and a flood, then an Adam.

Many of these small topics have had hundreds of volumes written on them. Better logic and proofs are available but exceed the purpose for this book.

If Christ did not exist, why does history record that ten of His friends asserted that He was the Son of God and were willing to die for that opinion?

Why does the world's dating system date back to the time of Jesus Christ? The year of my birth 1944 A.D. actually references two births His and mine.

The purpose of evolution as a religion is to eliminate the need for God so that man could more comfortably live outside of the authority of God.

We rest one day in seven, 'cause God said so. Remember the Sabbath day and keep it holy? Why do we not have a four-day week or a nine-day week? Is the number of days in a week a carry over from Genesis of six thousand years ago and one of God's commandments?

Is not creation by God obvious and well-supported?

Is not the existence and authority of God obvious?

37

History Of The World
In One Lesson

Where does the Christmas spirit come from? Not from Rudolph, Santa or Frosty the Snowman for sure. Christmas spirit first appeared long before any of these familiar characters of this season.

Creation...

Actually, Christmas spirit began several thousand years ago when God created the world. He created the earth, which had no sense of right and wrong. Then He created animals, which have instinct but no sense of right and wrong.

Then God created man, giving him a spirit and a sense of right and wrong, and a choice, making him very different from the animals

When God started, He had one simple rule which differentiated man from animals: "You will not eat from the tree in the center of the garden, called the tree of the knowledge of good and evil."

Man chose to sin against God and eat from that tree. The man, Adam, then became knowledgeable about sin. Once sin entered the world, everything went downhill, becoming worse and worse. Death, pain, and suffering originated at that time.

At first, men lived over 900 years (e.g. Adam, Seth, Methuselah). Then, as sin became more prevalent, lives became shorter. Fights among men became commonplace; in fact, Adam's son, Cain, killed his brother, Abel. God realized that man couldn't live without destroying himself so He gave man more rules.

Rules...

The next set was called *The Ten Commandments*. God knew that they would work for a little while, but that man would try to find ways around them. God wrote the books of Leviticus, Numbers and Deuteronomy to help men know how to live. God instituted a system of sacrifices for sin which men were required to make on a regular basis. These sacrifices were a way for man to say with sincerity, "I will give my best asset, a pure calf, a pure lamb, to express my sorrow for my disobedience to God."

That continued for about two thousand years until God knew it was time to send to earth the best and final solution for sin and disobedience.

Because He is just and fair, God had to have penalty for sin. For the quantity of sin prevalent in society two thousand years ago and still today, the only sacrifice big enough to cover the sin of man was God's own son, Jesus Christ. Jesus Christ, born as a man, but still fully God Himself, left heaven, came to earth, lived as we do on Earth, and was Himself nailed to a cross as the sacrifice to pay the penalty for our sins. This is so that we may spend eternity in Heaven with our Creator.

Jesus, the baby in the manger, the Son of God, gave Himself to become the Savior of the world.

This is the true Christmas spirit: Jesus giving up His home in heaven, living among men, dying on a cross for us, making possible our spending eternity in heaven. May we, at Christmas, be living examples of that Christmas spirit as we give of our lives and love to each other. Our gift giving is a symbol of the gift that God gave to us.

And now you know the rest of the story.

38

Bridge Builder and Analysis

The Bridge Builder
Will Allen Dromgoole

An old man, going a lone highway,
Came at the evening, cold and gray,
To a chasm vast and deep and wide;
The old man crossed in the twilight dim,
The sullen stream had no fear for him;
But he turned when safe on the other side,
And built a bridge to span the tide.

"Old man," said a fellow pilgrim near,
"You are wasting your strength in building here;
Your journey will end at the ending day,
You never again will pass this way;
You have crossed the chasm deep and wide;
Why build you this bridge at evening tide?"

The builder lifted his old gray head —
"Good friend, in the path I have come," he said,
"There followeth after me today,
A youth whose feet must pass this way;
This chasm that was naught to me
To that fair-haired youth may a pitfall be;
He, too, must cross in the twilight dim–
Good friend, I am building this bridge for him."

Analysis of poem:

I inserted this poem because it provides a great insight into our present problem.

The trick is to identify each component and symbolism in the poem.

The **old man** is **us**.

The **twilight** is **near the end of life**,

The **swollen stream** is the **obstacle** that will probably drown the next generation.

The **other side** is the **continuation of life,** safety, and Heaven.

The **fair-haired youth** is **anyone younger** with less knowledge, wisdom, experience, and fewer resources than the old man. There is a clear distinction; the youth was provided a bridge which he probably could not build himself. He was not provided an air-conditioned car to drive across.

Greatest Gift...

The greatest gift I can give to any fair-haired youth is the same political, religious, and economic liberty that I have enjoyed. Liberty to choose one's own government and how much of it and to speak freely about it. Freedom to accept or reject Christ and the practice of one's own religion. The opportunity to buy or sell, to hire or fire, to work or to leisure. We were once great believers in freedom. We joined the Young Americans for Freedom. We could not stand the bondage of slavery. We would not accept the chains of slavery in exchange for a little peace and security.

These conditions in America are not as perfect and complete as I would hope, but many places in the world have nothing approaching this level of freedom.

> **The greatest gift I can give to any fair-haired youth is the same political, religious, and economic liberty that I have enjoyed.**

You will notice the Bridge builder did not provide sports cars, tennis courts, or arenas for the amusement of the youth; he helped to solve an infrastructure problem. Motivated, intelligent people tend to focus their help in the form of permanent and long-term solutions, capital equipment so to speak, rather than relieving a short-term need.

39

Analysis of Ethical Systems by Which to Judge a Supplier

The pivotal issue in customer service is the underlying philosophical, ethical and moral values of the supplier. The underlying values will determine the actions you can expect.

What determines the values a person or company holds? What causes a decision to be made? What determines right and wrong? Do right and wrong change as determined by changes in the majority, law or the culture. Are there absolutes?

Answer these questions properly and you can predict what a company or person will do in most situations.

Many problems of life and business affect many different people: the customer, the employees, the stockholders, the neighbors, and the world as a whole. What is in the best interest of some may not be in the best interest of others. The profit of one may be the loss of another.

> **The humanist is usually driven by his own self righteousness and feels that he has the best view of what should be done by everyone else.**

There are basically two systems of ethics. One grouping is based on the Humanistic philosophy, the other Eternalistic.

The Humanistic philosophy of ethics.

The humanist asserts that there are no absolutes. He asserts that we evolved, that there is no God, and that man must determine for himself what is right and wrong. What is wrong today may be right tomorrow in his eyes. To him everything is relative. Consistency of values is impossible. If he bases his values on the laws, he must acknowledge that many laws are passed by a small majority and sometimes the majority oppresses the minority. Sometimes the powerful oppress the weak. The humanist is usually driven by his own self righteousness and feels that he has the best view of what should be done by everyone else. He often feels that the ends justify the means. He is Pragmatic. A bottom line type of person or company will determine that anything that increases profitability, especially short term, is the appropriate thing to do.

The Eternalistic philosophy of ethics.

The Eternalist says that there are absolutes. And we were created in the image of God. In addition, we have been given by him the guidelines for living. These guidelines are sometimes in stark contrast to those of the Humanist. This system of ethics, based on Eternal values, has God as the authority. Understanding that man did not know what to do or how he should live, God wrote a simplified law.

What were those commandments?

1 I am the Lord your God...you must have no other gods before me.
2. You must not make any idols.
3. You must not use the name of the Lord your God wrongly.
4. Remember the Sabbath Day, to keep it holy.
5. Honor your father and your mother.
6. You must not murder.
7. You must not commit adultery.
8. You must not steal.
9. You must not lie.
10. You must not covet anything that is your neighbor's."

These ten rules had been the basis for laws of the United States for many years.

Translating these laws into a set of personal and corporate values is important because values ultimately shape goals and daily operation practices. Businesses can not be operated in a moral vacuum. Parties doing business must assume moral values and principles such as honesty and good faith. They must assume that contracts will be honored.

On the Jefferson Memorial in Washington, D.C., are written these words that Jefferson wrote: "God who gave us life gave us liberty. Can the liberties of a nation be secure when we have removed a conviction that these liberties are the gift of God?" It is clear that Jefferson's America was based on the concept of God-given rights grounded in God-given moral rules called "Nature's Laws."

There is a universal social need for some natural moral principles by which conduct can be governed. Even apart from belief in God, natural law is necessary for ruling human societies.

Natural law can be summed up by the Golden Rule: "Do unto others as you would like them to do unto you."

Natural law is not hard to understand; it is just hard to practice. We know what we want others to do for us, even if we do not always want to do the same for them.

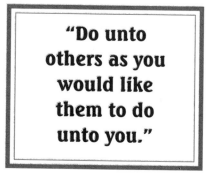

"Do unto others as you would like them to do unto you."

The natural law opposes an "end justifies any means" ethic on both a private and public level. This is particularly applicable in a capitalistic business context in which the profit motive is so dominant. Capitalism without moral values is destructive of society. It feeds on greed, produces injustice, and leads to revolution and war. Universal moral restraints, such as the natural law, are necessary to keep capitalism in check. Otherwise, money becomes the end goal. Moral principles are sacrificed for monetary profit.

Natural law is best summarized in the Ten Commandments in the Bible. Christians believe that the Bible is the word of God and is the only eternal and non-changing value base available to mankind. Since God created human beings, He also gave instructions as to how we should live with each other. The Ten Commandments summarize His guidance.

Business Ethics...

Business ethics can be defined as the application of values in the business world. Again, companies doing business must assume general moral principles, such as honesty and good faith. Companies, employees, suppliers, and customers must assume promises will be kept and contracts honored. If business is not conducted ethically, then many problems develop:

▲ Contracts are not honored

▲ Customers are not happy with products or services

▲ Needs of society are not met

▲ Employees are not treated properly

▲ Standard of living declines

▲ Economy becomes dysfunctional

If business is conducted in an ethical manner, lower cost of doing business results.

The character of an organization, such as a company, is a reflection of the people who make up the organization. If the people are honest and trustworthy, then the company will also be.

Application to business...

1. Show proper respect for authority.

"I am the Lord, your God ... you shall have no other gods before Me." Exodus 20:2,3

The absence of authority results in disorder. Showing proper respect for authority ensures order and a climate which encourages the proper functioning of the marketplace.

It is necessary to show proper respect for authority whether it is superior, subordinate, or on a peer level with you. Since God has vested His authority in our local, state, and national governments, and in our family and corporate life, all such authority merits and deserves proper respect. Proper exercise of authority is the invisible support structure of productive enterprise. It brings order from chaos.

When properly exercised, authority can give a sense of stability and purpose. Most leaders who are liked are respected for their proper exercise of authority. They are confident, visionary, and strong, yet also sensitive to their followers' needs. Proper authority involves justice and compassion, confidence and humility. It results in a respect that is earned, not commanded. The authority of God is an example of this.

> **Proper authority involves justice and compassion, confidence and humility.**

When improperly exercised, authority can create chaos instead of order. All of us know of people who exercise authority in the wrong way. Many times ego, power, and prestige are the motivating factors for someone to seek authority. This does not cause one to want to follow and obey what such a leader says.

2. Have a singleness of purpose.

"You shall not make for yourself an idol ..." Exodus 20:4

Effectiveness comes from activity focused on achieving a single purpose. Divided purposes dilute effectiveness when interests conflict. No individual or company can operate effectively while serving two masters.

Singleness of purpose involves the use of time, talent, and resources toward satisfying the needs of the customer. The needs of the customer must be the central focus of the supplier, not his own self interests.

3. Communicate appropriately and respectfully.

"You shall not misuse the name of the Lord your God..." Exodus 20:7

God's name should only be used in a statement of respect for God. The same should apply to our statements to people. Speak courteously and respectfully to everyone around you. It is my mouth that gets me into trouble. It is my mouth's words that issue false, demoralizing, destructive, disrespectful, pessimistic, hateful, sad, bitter, impatient, harsh and arrogant statements. Effective communication means the intended message is received, interpreted, and returned to the initiator with a meaning and spirit consistent with his intent. It is a responsibility that both the sender of the message and the receiver must work at.

Keeping your word, in the broad sense, means keeping promises, pledges, and oaths. This includes simple verbal commitments like being on time, or more complex commitments like written contractual agreements. It is a statement of intent with commitment and belief that the promise will be kept, and that an accurate description of the transaction will be given.

Spoken and written words have a specific meaning and are not arbitrary. In the simplest form, saying "yes" means yes, and saying "no" means no. It means doing what you say you will do, even if it is uncomfortable or inconvenient. It means telling the truth. It means that descriptions of products and services are consistent with performance. It means operating with these same expectations for others.

Complete communication and predictable follow-through are the basic expressions of personal integrity and the glue of profitability.

Suppliers, sellers, buyers, and servicers are all parts of the team which contribute to the integrity of a product or service. Each must perform his role to meet the expectation understood by the others. Exercise the courage to "understate and overproduce" whatever your role may be.

4. Provide proper rest, recreation, and reflection.

"Remember the Sabbath Day by keeping it holy." Exodus 20:8

Proper rest, recreation, and reflection are a hallmark of free men and free enterprise. They are a celebration of the privileges of free and responsible men under God. They are requirements for maximized creativity, productivity, and motivation. Rest is a necessity for effectiveness. Recreation clears the mind and guards against mental and emotional fatigue. Reflection "closes the loop" by which meaning is pressed into work and ensures single-mindedness.

Knowledge, creativity, productivity, and commitment of employees are directly related not only to their health, but to proper rest, recreation, and reflection.

5. Show respect for elders.

"Honor your father and mother so that you might live long ..." Exodus 20:12

Parents made your life possible. Their experiences can help their children avoid many pitfalls in life. If we do not learn from the mistakes of the previous generation, we are destined to repeat them. Ignore the warnings of parents, and we will generally have much more pain going through life. Rebellion against parents as well as rebellion against God virtually assures a society of experiencing pain.

6. Show respect for human life, dignity, and rights.

"You shall not murder." Exodus 20:13

Our Declaration of Independence contains the phrase, "We hold these truths to be self evident that men are endowed by their Creator with certain inalienable rights, that among them are life, liberty, and the pursuit of happiness. The lives of the unborn, the very old and every one in between are the greatest gifts of God. Man is the most important creation of God. It is self evident that God

Historically, where the family has been recognized and respected, the culture has enjoyed stability and longevity.

gave man life. Anyone who does not respect the value of someone else' s life can not be trusted to respect anything else including contracts, agreements, and the property of others.

7. Till death do us part.

"You shall not commit adultery." Exodus 20:14

Faithfulness to your marriage partner is fundamental to success of the family unit. The family functions best when husbands take final responsibility for their wives and love them without condition, when wives respect their husbands, and when children honor their parents.

Marriage and singleness have equally honorable status. A publicly committed marriage of a man to a woman is a desirable tradition. Children are a desirable benefit of that union and an invaluable asset to the relationship. The family unit is a greenhouse for growing commitment, convictions, communications, companionship, and a personal value system.

The foundational institution to every culture and society is the family unit. Historically, where the family has been recognized and respected, the culture has enjoyed stability and longevity. When the sexual uniqueness and responsibilities of men and women have been ignored or perverted, the culture has failed.

A person in business is faced with a crucial and fragile management issue. Respect for the family structure and the unique responsibilities of men as husbands and women as wives is a prerequisite for long-term profitability, even when current business demands seem to compete with family and personal life.

Every individual has the fundamental priority and responsibility for a strong home life.

Management decisions involving workload, deadlines, quotas, travel scheduling, etc., should be made in light of personal, marriage, and family needs.

When I married my first wife Sandy in 1965, we had typical unrealistic optimism about our futures. Little did we realize that the mid-eighties would have me experience three open heart surgeries, one of which left me paralyzed waist down for weeks. But Sandy was there. In the early nineties there were over a hundred days in which she never could get out of bed from the cancer that finally took her life.

Wedding vows include the phrases promising loyalty in better or worse, richer or poorer, in sickness or in health, till death do us part. Everybody does the right thing when it is easy. Everybody is faithful when everything is going the right way. God's standard is measured by such questions as, "What do you do when it is very hard. What do you do when no one is looking, and there is no way for anyone to find out? What do you do when it is no longer fun? What do you do when there is seemingly no benefit to you to keep your commitment?"

You measure the person or company by how well they perform when it is no longer in their own best interest to keep their promises.

8. Property rights are basic and fundamental.

"You shall not steal." Exodus 20:15

The stealing of company property, money, or assets results in reduced profitability, lower wages, increased prices to customers or some combination thereof. In addition, the thief loses self respect and becomes unproductive. He will experience a loss of trusted friendship. Some feel that cheating on income tax is not really theft. But it is. Remember, those who will steal for you will some day steal from you. About half of the people whom I have fired since being in business has been for theft.

9. Demonstrate honesty and integrity.

"You shall not give false testimony ..." Exodus 20:16

Business contracts. Business cannot function unless you can trust that a business contract will be fulfilled.

Advertising. If your product or service does not meet the advertised expectations, then your customers will not be happy and may not buy from you anymore. You simply can not promise more than you intend or are able to deliver. You do not put the good apples on top while the rotten ones are covered up.

Product quality. You should try to have a quality product or service so your customers will be happy. If you have a good reputation, developed through honesty and integrity, then customers will continue to buy from you. However, if you produce a bad quality product, even though you have a good reputation, then you are in effect lying to them about the quality

Personal reputation. You must guard against saying things which are degrading to fellow employees, customers and acquaintances. The theft of reputation is as

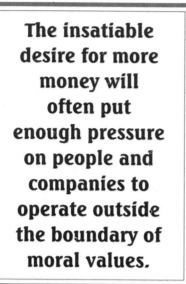

The insatiable desire for more money will often put enough pressure on people and companies to operate outside the boundary of moral values.

bad as the theft of property.

10. Maintain the right of ownership of property.

"You shall not covet ..." Exodus 20:17

Greed must not be the primary reason for being in business. Making a profit is a necessary and appropriate activity, but it must not be the determinant of personal or corporate values. The love of money is the root of all evil. The insatiable desire for more money will often put enough pressure on people and companies to operate outside the boundary of moral values.

Treatment of employees. Employees should be able to trust what they are told such as compensation amount, hours worked, and promotion criteria. If the employees are treated well and can trust what they hear, then they will enjoy their jobs more and be more motivated to perform good work resulting in happier customers.

No amount of ethical concerns and spiritual preaching will accomplish a more humane society unless the basic facts of creation, of God's mind and purposes, and of the human creative reality are respected. Without that, only sorrow and common poverty will result. Much of the world is a tragic living example of such poverty.

Biblically, different results, as consequences of different choices, would always serve as a form of judgment and lead in certain cases to improvement, adjustments, and renewed realism!

"If a man will not work, he shall not eat" (2 Thessalonians 3:10) describes this well. Truth should be discovered in reality. Consequences should not be kept from originally false or unrealistic choices. The market of reality in God's creation serves well as a testing ground for the truth or falsehood of any proposition. It is not the idea of justice in wealth distribution that brings wealth to a nation. Only hard work, skill, family relations and, where necessary, neighborly love will work toward a solution of scarcity problems.

In Biblical times, distribution of wealth was protected through the existence of one law and the availability of courts to protect the individual against those in power or the envy of his neighbors. Contracts could be made and were protected. Fines were set and bribes forbidden. Neither the poor nor the rich were to be treated with an advantage. All titles to property could be sold and the money reinvested differently. All commodities could be exchanged. Such an open system without market controls, enforced trading groups, or legal restraints gave the greatest breadth of possibilities for personal economic advantage through effort, skill, and adaptability

Rewarding excellent workers. Those people who are disciplined, creative, prudent, and work hard are entitled to the results of their work.

The value of human life and the worth of the individual demand morally right attitudes and actions. The responsibilities of the employer include product quality and service, work environment, and customers and employees' health and safety. The value of human life and the worth of the individual are the underlying issues of the anti-trust laws which guard against big business taking advantage of small business.

The concept may be as simple as living by the "Golden Rule" — treating people as you would want to be treated.

Application to business...

The Application of the Golden Rule, "do unto others as you would have them do unto you," is the fundamental basis for decision making in all relationships and management practices.

All operations should be conducted in a manner which protects the health and safety of all people. This extends to adequate instructions and training for production as well as for product use or service. Compliance with laws and regulations is a foundation from which the company should operate. Meeting minimum legal requirements does not guarantee an optimal work environment; the company should go beyond these minimums when appropriate.

Personnel policy and practice should be established with the view that all individuals are unique: unique combinations of skills, personality, talents, motivations, character, experience, and values. All of the uniqueness must be addressed for effective management and the optimal match of people with tasks.

Character, competence, and dedication, demonstrated on a sustained basis, should be rewarded and honored. Employees should treat each other in a way that creates harmony between labor and management.

> **If I must violate God's Law to stay in business, then I will choose to do something else.**

Biblical Basis for Ethics

The use of God's eternal Law for determining moral basis and ethical conduct does not guarantee financial maximization or success in this life.

My personal position is that I will operate my business on God's Laws the best I can and am able to understand. If I prosper, that is good. If I do not, that is okay, too. If I must violate God's Law to stay in business, then I will choose to do something else.

40

Can You Take It With You?

▲ I have explained that everyone whom we contact is a customer.

▲ I have given examples of good customer service.

▲ I have given examples of bad customer service.

▲ I have told you some of my life's experiences which led me to understand God's plan.

▲ I have explained how God's plan relates to customer service.

If you have accumulated more than is necessary to complete your life on Earth, "What are you going to do with your stuff?"

Can you take it with you?...

Who will decide, government or you?

Upon your death, government will dispose of all your stuff as it sees fit unless you predetermine the disposition of your stuff. Therefore, if you have faith in government and its values and its efficiency and are willing to have your stuff taxed again, then read no further. Government and the courts will be happy to dispose of your stuff for you.

When should the decisions be made?

You do it now, or government will do it later. You had the pleasure of making the money; you deserve the pleasure of seeing it do something good.

What stuff can you buy with cash?

I contend that you must either buy stuff for yourself or spend it on other people.

You have all the toys that you have time to play with... cars you do not have time to drive. You have been to nearly everywhere you wanted to go and continue to go. You have acquired all the stuff you wish to maintain, insure, learn to operate, and have under foot. Each item you buy complicates your life and puts more stuff in your way. Some of it gives pleasure for a while and then the void that was temporarily filled soon reappears.

Now what? Memorials? Tombstones? Yes, you want to be remembered and revered.

Cheops of Egypt (or whoever built the large pyramid on the southwest side of Cairo) built a tombstone that reportedly required a staff of twenty thousand people and twenty years to construct. If you build larger, you will be remembered for laying down a large pile of rock, too. Two problems: do you want your body to be over run with tourists? And do you really care about having the largest tombstone in the world?

> **Do you really care about having the largest tombstone in the world?**

Assuming not, what else can you do with your stuff?

Since you can not take it with you, the only real choice is that you give to your customers, the people whose lives you have responsibility to improve.

To whom do you have responsibility?

... to yourself. "Should we experience a loss of cabin pressure, a door will open above your head, exposing a mask. Take the mask and place it securely on your nose and mouth, and breathe normally. Should you be sitting with a small child, please secure your own mask and then assist the child." Dean Trulear said, " I used to wonder why do I have to put my own mask on first and then the kid's, until I flew with my children ten years ago. When I flew with them; I realized that in the back of my mind, if something happened to the plane, my first instinct as a parent would be to take care of my children, to make sure that they got their oxygen. What the airline understands is that while I'm busy working to get my three children's masks on, I could pass out and then all of us are in trouble. So what the airline is saying is put your own mask on first. You have a God-given responsibility to care for yourself. If you do not take care of yourself, you can do no good for anyone else. With God's mercy, you will live to age 75. You should set aside enough assets to maintain your standard of living. You worked for it; you deserve it. God approves of wealth accumulation and condemns idleness, laziness, and unprofitability. In Scripture, references to work are found hundreds of times; however, there seems to be no mention of retirement.

...to your parents. God said, "Honour thy father and thy mother: that thy days may be long upon the land which the LORD thy God giveth thee." Obviously providing for the sustenance of one' s own parents clearly falls into the category of honoring them.

...to your wife. You have made a pledge "'til death do us part." Paul said a man should "love his wife as Christ did the church and gave himself for it." You have the obligation to care for your wife throughout her life as well as you provide for your own future.

...to your children. You have raised them, taught them to work, and provided as much as they would take of education to equip them for their futures. What more can you do than give them tools? Quite sadly, sometimes, the more you help, the more dependent and less motivated they become. One does not want to see his children suffer. However struggle is a very good thing. If we as parents could purchase happiness, independence, self-reliance, security, eternal life, peace, freedom, and other good things for our children, we would probably do it. It is fun to give wonderful gifts to those you love. We can provide some sort of safety net/comfort nest for them, but the remainder must be recognized, appreciated, desired and sought after by each individual. To the extent a safety-net/comfort-nest provides a higher launch pad for greater achievements, it is probably a good thing. To the extent it generates indulgence, dependence and apathy, it is probably a bad thing. A beautiful butterfly had to emerge from its cocoon from the caterpillar stage. If it were helped to make its emergence painless, it would not have developed the necessary strength for survival as a butterfly.

...to your employees. Some cultures have the principle of maintaining the employee/employer relationship for life. In America it is not so. In small industries we promise to pay employees each week for what they do and provide them with health insurance, but their future is, by agreement, their responsibility. We might do a better job of helping some that are not as foresighted as we are to understand life better, but it is not our business to provide them with lifelong security, comfort and ease.

...to **Alma Maters, associations, clubs, trade associations, community, country and world.** They are logically the same thing. They are simply groups of people distinguished by demography, geography, or common interest.

...**to Earth.** In the sense of environment, natural resources, trees, ozone, oil and whales, none of these matter unless there are people to enjoy them.

Needs of People

There is a spectrum in the needs of people. There is need for relief, consumption, capital, infrastructure, education, and ideology.

...**Relief.** If there is a need for such as clothing, food, or warmth then it may be appropriate to help by providing relief from that suffering.

...**Consumption.** Providing things to people to increase their standard of living may simply increase their level of consumption and comfort. Sometimes that is helpful and sometimes hurtful. Does it create independence or dependence?

...**Capital.** Capital is the means of production. It may be factory buildings, machinery, or things that are directly involved in the production of a product.

...**Infrastructure.** The hardware of the very basic needs of a community to do anything. Roads, dams, water, telephone service are part of infrastructure.

...**Education.** Facts and information.

...**Ideology.** The moral and basic knowledge of a nation and people which provide it with goals, values and principles upon which to base its laws and code of ethics for daily living.

I believe that I must help people by giving understanding of the best ideology in the world, the knowledge of Jesus Christ as Savior of the world along with knowledge of His teachings of how to live.

What Can I Give to My Customers?

▲ My greatest gift to others is knowledge of eternal life provided by Jesus Christ.

▲ My second greatest gift is religious liberty.

▲ My third greatest gift is economic liberty.

▲ My fourth greatest gift is political liberty.

These gifts bundle well as a package. My strategy therefore is to find people who are willing to become salesmen and promoters of the above gifts. These generally are teachers and missionaries. The cost of communication within America is extremely high compared to the rest of the world. Americans are inundated with advertising, information and messages of all sorts. The remainder of the world is quite different, however. Many of the world's people have, at least until recently, been behind the Iron Curtain. They were prevented from freedom of worship, speech, assembly and owning property.

The most receptive place for teachers and missionaries to operate is behind the former

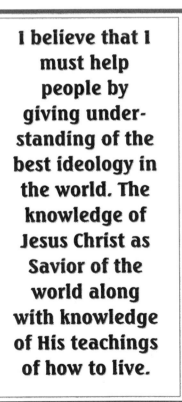

I believe that I must help people by giving under-standing of the best ideology in the world. The knowledge of Jesus Christ as Savior of the world along with knowledge of His teachings of how to live.

Iron Curtain where knowledge of the above four gifts was almost completely non-existent for centuries.

Between 1968 and 1989 if you tried to escape from East Germany, you would be shot in the back. In the mid-1930's if you were a Ukrainian, you had a high probability of being one of the 35,000,000 people starved to death by your soviet masters. In the 1930's and 40's you stood a good chance of being one of 6,000,000 experiencing an Auschwitz-style gas oven if you were a Jew. As a black slave in America in 1750, your income tax rate was 100%. As an American now, the tax rate is 40%.

Where the slave master dictators dominated is the area with the easiest sell and greatest receptivity of a new ideology. There is a vacuum of ideas behind the former Iron Curtain. Where there is a vacuum, filling is most efficient and cost effective. There is much less clutter with competing ideology or other advertising.

I find compulsory servitude highly repulsive; while I find voluntary servitude beautiful.

That is why I have spent substantial time and money over the last several years helping to fund people who teach business ethics, philosophy, world history, Christian theology, psychiatry, and law. All this is to help a people learn how to live at peace with each other and with their Maker.

Vietnam, China, Siberia, Russia, Romania, United States, Czech Republic, Ukraine, Uzbekistan, Nicaragua, Slovakia ...wherever, the objective is the same. To convey the values of liberty and Christianity to people who would not otherwise have the opportunity to learn them.

To help relieve a person's current problem has always been a temptation to me. I know that I must focus on ideology... how the people think. If people think right, the problems relating to oppression, aristocracy, poverty, discrimination, theft, and crimes will probably diminish.

Without an underlying Christian worldview, there is little hope of solving the remainder of the problems. Too much time is spent fighting the problems of society, be they theft, drugs, assault, or poor customer service. The root cause is an impure heart. A Christian relationship to God will solve more problems than we can describe in this short volume. I want the world to have a Christian worldview. I want it to think freedom; I want it to think Christianly.

> **If people think right, the problems relating to oppression, aristocracy, poverty, discrimination, theft, and crimes, will probably diminish.**

Thus it is my desire to concentrate on ideological education rather than the consumptive good of relief.

A closing thought

On a cold wintry night in northern Canada a man nearly frozen to death and lost came upon an old cabin. He entered and found only a note. "Make yourself at home. Warm yourself by the fire. Stay as long as you like. Leave a higher stack of wood than you found."

The stack of wood, of course, is our personal liberty. Patriots have fought, bled and died for our freedom. I intend to do what I can to leave more people free in the world than I found.

God said, "It is more blessed to give than to receive." I want to be known as one who gave knowledge of spiritual, economic and political freedom to my customers.

Many thanks to:

Cliff Schimmels who said, "Just write it." Cliff and his wife, Mary, actually spent a whole weekend helping to get this project off the ground.

Strategists: **Shawn Loy** and **Brian Burnett**

Philosophical advisors: **David Hoover, Dennis Miller, Charlie Phillips** and **Rick Purde**

Website designer: **Matt LaMaster**

Editors: **Anne Coates** and **Becky Byars**

Readers: **Lester** and **Brenda Lee, Cliff** and **Mary Schimmels, Dan Smith, Marshall** and **Sara Cherry, Alan Myers, Jeff Hougland,** and **Wesley Jackson**

Other sterling examples of character in this book: **Mildred Coates, Elizabeth Allen, Sarah** and **Chris Graham**

Encouragers: **Steve** and **Michelle Gibbs, Mark Byars**

Artists along the way: **Judy Lewis** and **Ray Bowling**

Photographers: **Kris Pedigo** and **Beth Albertson**

Computer guru: **Randy Allen**, who kept the computers and printers running

Typists: **Elizabeth Allen** and **Anne Coates**

The folks at Country Pines Printing: **Wilma Albright, Eloise Haycox** and all their helpers

My wife, **Anne**, who read, re-read and re-re-read, drove, flew, waited, hosted and patiently slept alone while I wrote until 5 a.m. many mornings.

Floyd Coates

Born 1944

Attended Virginia Military Institute and Hanover College, receiving a Bachelor's degree in physics.

President and owner of American Plastic Molding Corp. (A custom injection molder of plastics) and Southern Mold and Tool Corp.

Member of Society of Plastics Engineers, Association of Union Bible College, board of International Institute for Christian Studies, and Chairman of the Taxpayers' Watchdog committee.

Coates is a former nominee for State Representative and U.S. Congress.

He is an instrument rated pilot, musician, and speaker on free enterprise, political and religious issues.

Coates is married to Anne and they live near Scottsburg, Indiana. They have four children and thirteen grandchildren!

For further information about the author or his company:

Floyd Coates

American Plastic Molding Corp.

965 South Elm St.

Scottsburg, IN 47170

Voice 1.812.752.7000

Fax 1.812.752.5155
e-mail to floyd@APMC.com

Or web site at www.apmc.com

Or web site at www.floydcoates.com

"American Plastic Molding is a custom injection molder of engineered plastic molded parts. Its plant is located in Scottsburg, Indiana. American specializes in product design, development, prototyping, mold building, molding and plastic part production. American is ISO-9000 certified and processes all grades of engineered plastic materials. Inquires are invited."

Floyd Coates, President